Carrier Strike Force

Pacific Air Combat in World War II

ERNEST A. McKAY

Illustrated

JULIAN MESSNER NEW YORK

Published by Julian Messner, a Simon & Schuster
Division of Gulf & Western Corporation,
Simon & Schuster Building,
1230 Avenue of the Americas,
New York, New York   10020.
JULIAN MESSNER and colophon are trademarks of
Simon & Schuster, registered in the U.S. Patent
and Trademark Office.
Manufactured in the United States of America.

Design by Irving Perkins Associates

Library of Congress Cataloging in Publication Data

McKay, Ernest A.
    Carrier strike force.

    Bibliography: p. 185
    Includes index.
    Summary: Describes the creation of a new
American carrier fleet in the Pacific following
the attack on Pearl Harbor and its success in
blocking enemy expansion and leading the attack on
Japan.
    1. World War, 1939-1945—Naval operations,
American—Juvenile literature.   2. Aircraft
carriers—United States—History—20th century—
Juvenile literature.   3. World War, 1939-1945—
Pacific Ocean—Juvenile literature.   [1. World War,
1939-1945—Naval operations, American.   2. World
War, 1939-1945—Pacific Ocean]   I. Title.   II. Title:
Pacific air combat in World War II.
D773.M36   940.54′5973   81-10996
ISBN 0-671-43127-7   AACR2

*Photos, courtesy Department of the Navy, Office of Information,
Photojournalism and Public Inquiries Branch, Washington, D.C.*

Acknowledgments

Special thanks are due Lieutenant Commander Arthur E. Norton, USN, and Robert A. Carlisle of the Navy Office of Information, and Jane R. Perlungher, Director of the Cold Spring Harbor Library, Cold Spring Harbor, New York. My wife Ellen helped with research and sound advice every step of the way, and my children's interest was a great lift.

Contents

1.

Defense to Offense

During World War II in the Pacific it is one year after the Japanese attack on Pearl Harbor. The American aircraft carriers are almost wiped out, but plans begin for a new offensive.

The Japanese enjoyed their revenge. Only a few months before, Jimmy Doolittle had shaken hands with Captain Mitscher on the carrier *Hornet* and then turned to his B-25 crews and said, "O.K. fellas, this is it! Let's go!" With full flaps, and motors at full throttle, they had taken off from the big carrier in the face of a gale to make the first air raid on Tokyo. Now, off Santa Cruz Island, protecting Guadalcanal, the *Hornet* reeled under the devastating attack of an enemy strike group.

Overhead, Wildcat fighters of the Combat Air Patrol dove to defend their ship with little effect. Lieutenant Al Pollock shot down one enemy plane, Ensign Steve Kona got another, and Ensign Don Gordon still another. But there were too many. The Japanese kept coming and their pilots skillfully zoomed in on the *Hornet* and scored solid hits. The wounded commander of one bombing squadron, ready to sacrifice his life for the Emperor, crashed into the carrier's flight deck with two bombs that created havoc. Fires raged throughout the ship as a torpedo plane smashed into the port bow.

Again and again, the Japanese struck. By early afternoon, the *Hornet* had taken six bombs, two torpedoes, two crashed

9

planes, and a number of damaging near-misses. And yet, the men of the *Hornet* did not give up. Firefighters, working desperately as flames and smoke swirled into the sky, were sure that they could save the ship. They were wrong.

Two hours later, eight Zeros and seven Kate torpedo bombers tackled the wounded carrier again. A torpedo opened up a hole in the engine room that gave the ship a sharp list and bombs pulverized the flight deck. It was hopeless. Charles Mason, now the captain of the *Hornet*, sadly ordered the ship abandoned.

The loss of the *Hornet* did not mean the loss of the battle of Santa Cruz, but it was possible that a greater loss had been inflicted. The Pacific fleet now had only one carrier capable of action. At this dark moment there was no doubt that the powerful Japanese Imperial Fleet had superior naval air power.

At the start of 1943, a little more than a year had passed since the surprise attack on Pearl Harbor. It had been a grim, defensive year. Wake Island, Guam, the Philippines, Singapore, and Java had all surrendered. The enemy threatened India to the west and Australia to the south.

After the destruction of much of the United States fleet on the "Day of Infamy," Navy men, in their dejection, had reassured each other with the thought that at least the aircraft carriers had survived. Luckily, they were at sea December 7, 1941. But the next twelve months had not been especially kind to the carriers.

The ungainly flattops, easy to identify from the air, were prime targets. They were also vulnerable. Their armor was thin, gun power was light, and storage tanks of high octane aviation fuel were potential torches that could blow the ship sky high. A damaged flight deck could halt the operation of dozens of aircraft, and a carrier without wings was a huge, harmless hulk.

During 1942, one carrier after another had gone down. The old *Langley*, the first commissioned carrier in the Navy, was sunk by land-based planes in the East Indies while serving as an aircraft tender with the Asiatic fleet. The *Lexington* went down in the battle of Coral Sea, and the *Yorktown* was lost at Midway. In the struggle for Guadalcanal, the *Saratoga* was hit for the second time in August, the *Wasp* was sunk by a Japanese submarine in September, and in October the *Hornet* received her fatal blows. In the battle off Santa Cruz, the *Enterprise* had taken a beating too. Three bombs ripped the flight and hangar decks and killed forty-four seamen. But the badly battered *Enterprise* kept her colors flying and by November was the only American carrier operating in the Pacific. As one of her admirers wrote, she was one of the few in the beginning and one of the many at the end.

It is frequently forgotten that aircraft carriers were an untried weapon before World War II. The primitive experiences of the British with carriers in World War I meant little in this new, complex conflict, and early in World War II British losses created deeper doubts. Their carriers, *Courageous, Ark Royal,* and *Hermes* were all at the bottom of the sea by the spring of 1942. It is no wonder that some proponents of air power, such as Alexander de Seversky, claimed that aircraft carriers were too easy to sink and that the way to win the war was with land-based aircraft.

In the dismal year of 1942, there were two important consolations for the United States. Despite disappointments

11

MIDWAY ISLAND

Pearl Harbor

HAWAIIAN ISLANDS

Wake

Kwajalein

MARSHALL ISLANDS

Makin

Tarawa

ISLANDS

PACIFIC OCEAN

OMON ISLANDS

NTA CRUZ ISLANDS

and serious reverses, the Navy had won a strategic victory in the first carrier battle of the war at Coral Sea, and a major air victory that turned the tide at Midway. The Navy wanted to move from the defensive to the offensive, but it had a long way to go and needed more ships, more planes, and more men.

Both sides took time to lick their wounds, rest, and rebuild their strength in 1943. In the United States, contrary to critics, construction of new carriers was underway. The nation was determined to show that her industrial might packed a wallop. In June, a new aircraft carrier, *Essex*, arrived in Pearl Harbor. It was the model for a class of ships that would give hope for better days to come. The next month, the light carrier *Independence* appeared in the Pacific. Sister ships of these two types would arrive at the rate of almost one a month. By the end of the war, sixteen *Essex* and nine *Independence* class carriers would face the enemy.

With this renewed strength, Admiral Ernest J. King, Chief of Naval Operations in Washington, D.C., wanted to put more pressure on the Japanese. No one who ever served under him doubted his determination as the number one admiral in the Navy. He was tough, sharp, and forthright. For years the tall, gaunt, seaman had operated on the principle that "a taut ship is a happy ship." Those who had the audacity to cross his path did so at their own peril.

Everyone agreed that the final goal was to reach Japan. Still, there were many roads to the enemy homeland. Burma, the Philippines, Marianas, Formosa, China, all presented possible routes. General Douglas MacArthur, a man of strong opinions, was certain that returning to the Philippines was an absolute necessity. He had given his promise when he said, "I shall return." Others were not so sure he was right.

Looking backward, the choices seem simple. Looking forward, the choices were complex and confused. Admiral Chester Nimitz, Commander-in-Chief of the Pacific Fleet, once said, "Hindsight is notably cleverer than foresight." It is a truism that everyone forgets. Monday morning quarterbacks are no help.

The new *Essex* carriers stirred the imagination of Navy commanders. They believed that the struggles of the Solomon Islands were behind them and that a new era had begun. Carriers could roam the great distances of the Pacific, control air and sea, strike quickly, and move to another target hundreds of miles away. Speed and mobility opened new vistas. Assaults could be made on strategic islands only, the others could be bypassed and left to die on the vine. This would be a game of leap frog that could shorten the war by months or years. That, at least, was the theory. Would it work in practice?

Eventually, uncertainties about objectives were cast aside. The time for decision arrived and Admiral King and other members of the Joint Chiefs of Staff set the strategy. Their two-pronged plan called for General MacArthur, commander of the forces in the southwest Pacific, to advance north from New Guinea toward the Philippines. Another advance under Admiral Nimitz, using the new fast carriers, was to move west from Pearl Harbor through the widely scattered islands of the central Pacific.

Nimitz remained at his headquarters at Pearl Harbor. The commander at sea was Vice Admiral Raymond Spruance. He had been brilliant at Midway when he served as a pinch hitter for his old friend, Bill Halsey, who was ill at the time. King thought Spruance had the best brains in the Navy. He had another characteristic in common with many of the best sailors of the past and the mythical Horatio Hornblower. He suffered from seasickness.

The Spruance reputation for clear thinking was well-founded. Past victories, however, can be quickly forgotten. It is always the next operation that counts. It was up to Spruance to grasp thousands of details, place them in perspective, and go into action.

The new carriers were called "fast" because they could cut through the sea at better than thirty knots. And they were accompanied by new battleships, cruisers, and destroyers that had speed, gunpower, and maneuverability to protect the carriers. They were the screen. Before long, the Fast Carrier Task Force in Spruance's fleet would have more than a hundred ships and carry about a hundred thousand men.

Tarawa in the Gilbert Islands was the target for the first operation for the new Fast Carrier Task Force. If successful, it would be the beginning of a campaign to penetrate the Japanese inner ring of defense that protected lines of communication for food, fuel, and critical raw materials. Japan needed these imports to live and fight, and many of them, such as oil and rubber, came from the rich Dutch East Indies. Survival and success depended upon the Japanese Imperial Fleet protecting this line. The American advance depended upon cracking that line. Sooner or later these two great fleets would meet again.

2.

The Fast Carriers

Speedy new American carriers, large as floating cities, appear in the Pacific and give new hope for the future.

Sailors like to give their ships nicknames. It reflects a sense of pride and sometimes a sense of humor. The old *Lexington* was "Lady Lex," the *Saratoga* was "Sara," and the *Enterprise* was, of course, the "Big E." The letter "E" had a special significance because a Navy E for efficiency was a coveted award and the crew of the *Enterprise* wanted everyone to know that she was tops. Referring to these great ships in such a casual manner also helped build a sailor's ego because it was a way of saying that he was a part of the best.

The new *Essex* class carriers that started to appear in Pearl Harbor by late summer of 1943 had not yet developed such character. Nicknames were missing. They were welcome additions to the fleet, but the green crews and green ships were still untested and unknown. Only the months ahead would prove, or disprove, their worth. Soon there would be plenty of tests.

The *Essex* and her sister ships were always described as large, but their size depended upon how you looked at them. In a drydock, they were mammoth. Alongside a destroyer, they were huge. In the air, looking down from above, things were different. If you were a pilot circling to

As one plane banks after takeoff, another can be seen leaving an *Essex* class carrier

make an approach in a rain squall, a rolling sea, or even the clearest day of the year, the *Essex* would seem to have shrunk. On the downwind leg, flying in the opposite direction of the carrier at an altitude of 250 feet, there would be time to wonder about your ability to land on an airfield that never stood still. Despite the best training in the world, you would know that operational hazards were almost as big a threat as the enemy. Then, gradually turning into the wind on the same heading as the carrier, there would be no time for hesitation. A hundred yards astern of the ship, about twenty or thirty feet above the flight deck, the speed would be about ten knots above stalling, the nose of the plane up, wheels and flaps down, and the LSO, landing signal officer, would come clearly into view. An experienced aviator, standing on a small platform, usually on the port side of the flight deck at the stern, he becomes all important. Split seconds count as he gives his decisive instructions.

The LSO holds a paddle in each hand for clear visibility and his signals become explicit instructions for the pilot to follow. A false judgment can mean disaster. His motions may tell you to speed up because you are coming in too slow, or slow down because you are too fast, or perhaps his hands are telling you that your landing hook is not down. If he crosses his arms over his head, you know the approach is no good and you must go around again. If his arms are outstretched to the sides, you can relax, everything is "O.K." The engine is cut, the landing hook latches onto the ship's arresting gear, and the plane comes to a stop with an abrupt jolt that throws you against the safety belt. You are safe aboard, and now the size of the carrier changes. Suddenly, it is huge again.

The landing signal officer directs a plane into a landing on board the *Nassau.*

Men in green jerseys quickly appear from the sides of the deck to detach the plane's landing hook. As you might expect, they are called "hookmen." Another seaman in a yellow shirt signals the pilot forward. He is the plane director and is anxious to make room for other planes about to land. There is plenty of moving color that leaves no question about who does what. Colors signify purpose. Communications men in brown are the "talkers" relaying orders, chockmen wear purple, the ever-ready firefighters are in red, and dozens of seamen are in the more normal blue shirts. Many of the deck crew wear bright linen helmets and gloves called "flash clothes." They are a mild protection against burns, an ever-present danger. There are also men in asbestos suits who look like they are ready to go to Mars standing by to fight any widespread fire. All their jobs are carefully synchronized, and all are important.

The deck that seemed so small was almost as long as three football fields. If stood on end, it would have been as tall as a seventy-story skyscraper. The *Essex* was 820 feet in length, and the extreme beam was 147 feet 6 inches. Her gunpower was far less than a battleship or cruiser, but she had twelve five-inch guns and a multitude of 40mm and 20mm antiaircraft guns to ward off enemy attackers. The geared turbines that drove her to a speed of thirty-two knots were 150,000 horsepower. On board were a hundred planes, the reason for her existence.

With all of the evidence of a modern air age on board the ship, there were contradictions that reminded all hands of the ancient ritual of the sea. The boatswain's pipe, used to keep Greek and Roman galley slaves in stroke, still came through the loudspeaker system loud and clear. It was usually a prelude to such mundane announcements as, "Sweepers man your brooms," or "The smoking lamp is out," which meant no smoking.

The Navy had a language of its own that did more than linger on. It was accepted by the youngest seaman. Rumors, for instance, which spread throughout the ship, as they did unceasingly, were always referred to as "scuttlebutt," a word that went back to sailing ships. And customs were equally well-entrenched and observed. Saluting the quarterdeck on coming aboard was only one of many such expressions of Navy life that remained unchanged for centuries.

Amidships, overlooking the flight deck, was the island structure that housed the command center for air and sea operations. High up in the gray tower was the bridge where the captain, officer of the deck, and helmsman sailed the ship. There, they scanned the sea, checked bearings, and marked on their minds the positions of other ships. Unlike most seamen, they also were concerned with flight and were especially sensitive to wind direction and velocity. When the time came for launching planes, they would carefully maneuver the ship into the wind. Coordination between seamen and airmen was fundamental.

A level below the ship's bridge was the flag bridge where an admiral would preside when aboard and the air officer directed flight operations. Inside, off the flag bridge, a staff duty officer kept vigil over the flag plot on a large chart table. It gave the location of ships of the fleet and estimated the position of the enemy based upon intelligence reports. It was a never-ending job for junior officers to keep up-to-date. The plot meant little to an inexperienced observer, but an admiral's glance could quickly spot critical data,

An F6F-3 fighter is readied for launch on the *Yorktown*. Note the target information written on the board seen under the propeller.

An Avenger being launched from a carrier.

interpret the meaning, and make rapid calculations about distances, speeds, and probable actions.

Boards on the bulkheads in flag plot gave the status of available aircraft, types of bomb loads, and times of launching. There were also radar repeaters that showed friendly and enemy ships and aircraft.

The officers in flag plot were in continual touch with the Combat Information Center (CIC) in the gallery deck which hung beneath the flight deck. CIC, with the help of radar, passed along facts about ship and aircraft locations and controlled the combat Air Patrol that protected the carrier overhead.

Still another section that worked closely with flag plot was intelligence. Their officers interpreted aerial photographs of enemy strongholds that might become targets. Others pulled together the most complete story possible about the enemy from the interrogation of pilots recently back from a mission.

The war was a confusing business and, despite every effort, information was always incomplete. An admiral who could grasp the situation with sketchy, and sometimes misleading, data would succeed. In many ways, it was a giant jigsaw puzzle with entirely too many pieces missing.

The fast carriers were often said to be floating cities and the comparison was justified. Crowded in a compact area, three thousand or so people spent their daily lives. In the city at sea they ate, slept, worked, prayed, and played. Serving their needs were specialists of every kind. As in any city, there were butchers and barbers, shoemakers and storekeepers.

Tons of meat and vegetables fed the hungry crowd. And

they were very well-fed. The Navy was proud of its graduates of the cooks and bakers school who prepared the thousands of meals each day. The enlisted men ate in shifts, cafeteria style, but rank had its privileges. The Navy, as always, was a hierarchy. There were separate dining rooms for chief petty officers, warrant officers, and commissioned officers. The executive officer of the ship, the second ranking member of the ship's company, was president of the commissioned officer's mess and everyone stood until he appeared in the wardroom and said, "Gentlemen, be seated." In war and peace it was important that an officer was a gentleman. Stewards in white coats waited on tables. The ship's captain and admiral each had their separate mess and invited whomever they pleased to dine with them.

PT boats, amphibious craft, and submarines may have had their attractions, but their cramped quarters left little space for refrigeration and storage for large quantities of supplies. Consequently, their menus would frequently suffer when they were at sea for long periods of time. Their crews had every reason to be jealous of the men on the carriers who rarely had such worries.

The big ships had other luxuries that smaller ships lacked. Perhaps most important were the medical facilities. A dentist, in his well-equipped office, could give regular checkups and care for the most painful toothache. A staff of medical doctors and corpsmen attended the sick and wounded in an elaborate hospital. A sudden case of appendicitis was never a problem. The patient was simply rolled into the spotless operating room for a surgeon to go to work.

When time allowed, the flight deck was just the place for a game of touch football, and the hangar deck was often a motion picture theater. On Sundays the hangar became a church. A chaplain led the divine services and on other days counseled those with personal problems. In a city this size there was bound to be a variety of heartaches. Frequently, problems at home added more to the sailor's worries at sea than the enemy, and the chaplain was always ready to help.

The main purpose of the hangar deck, as the name implied, was to store and repair aircraft. When ready for flight, an enormous outboard elevator moved the planes to the flight deck. The elevator was the ship's Achilles heel. If the elevator was damaged by the enemy, the ship was practically paralyzed. The dimensions of the elevator and the flight deck also had an influence on the design of aircraft. The space limitations were the reasons for folding wings and the way they were folded. Space was at a premium.

On the hangar deck aviation mechanics worked long hours to keep the planes flying. Around the deck technicians of all kinds were busy climbing all over planes making repairs and adjustments. The noise was incessant. Overhead could be heard the roar of launching and landing of aircraft, and in the hangar could be heard the hammering and banging of metal workers and mechanics, and a hundred other irritations to the ear. Machine shops hummed away. Spare parts were packed in every possible nook.

Gasoline, oil, sweat, and grease permeated the air and probably reminded more than one worker of the resemblance to his hometown service station. Fuel storage, however, was considerably larger. Hundreds of thousands of gallons of high octane gasoline, always a hazard, were stored in tanks, as well as millions of gallons of fuel oil to run the ships.

F6Fs ready for takeoff on the deck of the *Yorktown.*

Carriers, as instruments of destruction, were loaded with ammunition of all kinds for the ship and planes. Tons of bombs of varying sizes, and 2,000-pound torpedoes were ready for ordnance men to wheel out in their one-handed barrows when the time came to arm the planes. The power was mighty, but it was a two-edged sword. A lucky enemy hit could create havoc in this arsenal.

On each fast carrier there was an air group with a squadron each of fighters, dive bombers, and torpedo planes. The squadrons of fighters were designated VF; the bombers, VB; the scout bombers, VSB; and the torpedo planes, VT. In the air, the squadron commander was supreme.

Unlike Japanese airmen who would often go into action with less than a hundred flying hours, Americans usually had five hundred hours of flight time and that was often the difference between life and death. By 1943, there were two well-trained air groups for each carrier and the pilots alternated to prevent combat fatigue.

The new aircraft that promised so much were on board. Would they live up to their promises?

The Japanese Zero, menace of the skies, had great speed and range. It was a light plane because the Japanese did not worry about extra protection for the pilot. The weight was put into fuel tanks that could give them greater distance. Built in a number of models, the Zero-sen or "Zeke" had a top speed of 330 miles per hour, a ceiling of 33,000 feet, and a fast climb that could reach 20,000 feet in about eight minutes.

The F6F Hellcat, specifically built to outmatch this Japanese terror, took the place of the F4F Wildcat that had done yeoman service in the early part of the war. Shortcomings or not, the Wildcat in the hands of a skillful pilot was an effective fighter. Actually, the F6F was simply a more powerful version of the Wildcat that incorporated lessons learned from earlier battles.

The Grumman Hellcat statistics gave hope for the future. It offered speed and a greater range. The maximum speed was 375 miles per hour, the range was better than a thousand miles, and the ceiling was 35,000 feet. Its ruggedness and simplicity were its beauty. When stowed aboard, the square-tipped wings neatly folded back alongside the fuselage. Optimism reigned when Navy fliers thought of the possibilities of this new addition.

The gull-winged F4U Corsair fighter offered more promises. Its speed was even greater. It had a speed of 446 miles per hour. Still, some thought of it as a land-based plane and it would take time to determine its effectiveness as a carrier aircraft.

Since the start of the war, torpedo bombers had failed to fulfill their expectations. Torpedo 8, operating from the *Hornet*, had been wiped out at Midway. It was a disaster that made commanders sensitive about their future use. Perhaps the fault was with tactics instead of design, but it left everyone apprehensive. Nevertheless, the Grumman TBF Avenger appeared as a replacement torpedo bomber. The fat-looking single-engine plane, when loaded, weighed nearly eight tons, but it had a speed of 270 miles per hour, almost a hundred miles per hour faster than the old TBD. Part of the speed came from almost a thousand extra horsepower in the Wright R-2600 engine. Wind resistance was cut down too, because the plane carried bombs internally.

The Avenger carried armament of five machine guns and

An Avenger in flight over the Pacific.

up to 2,000 pounds of bombs, or one 1,920-pound torpedo, or eight rockets. The crew of three fitted in the canopied greenhouse above the wing. The heavy plane had the defensive and offensive qualities of a twin-engine aircraft. Perhaps the TBF would change opinions about torpedo bombers.

Less optimism surrounded the Curtiss SB2C Helldiver. It was intended to replace the SBD dive bomber that had gained everyone's respect. The new model came along because some experts believed that the SBD was rapidly becoming outdated. Others differed. Many pilots were confident that there was still plenty of life in the old SBD. It was a name synonymous with precision bombing, which was what dive bombers were all about. There were good reasons for misgivings about the Helldiver. It had to be admitted that there had been production problems, and tests almost condemned the Helldiver at the start. The biggest trouble was lack of stability. Was it stable enough now to do the job in combat?

The success or failure of the new fast carriers would go hand in hand with the fate of these four new planes.

Before launching and after landing, pilots would be seen in their ready rooms. There they would be briefed before takeoff on the day's mission, the weather, enemy situation, and other operational matters. While the pilots waited for briefings there was never a hint of their inner thoughts. Some quietly played cribbage or acey-deucey to pass the time. Others had lively conversations about girl friends or their most recent episodes ashore.

Upon returning, the pilots would be "debriefed" to learn what had happened. Often, intelligence officers waited for the fliers to pick up a can of pineapple juice or a sandwich at the canteen before the questions began. Debriefing was a delicate job. Questioning tired pilots who were under strain was necessary, but it required diplomacy.

Routine on board ship frequently turned into boredom, and every day every man wished the war would end so he could go home. Still, the days did not drag. Time sped quickly in the Pacific as one day dissolved into another. In reality days never ended on board ship. It was a twenty-four-hour-a-day job for the ship handlers, and even the Air Department found that the day started early and ended late.

A normal day for the Air Department would begin with reveille at 0400, long before sunrise. Thirty minutes later, the Combat Air Patrol would be launched. At 0500, pilots and crewmen would be at flight quarters, and by 0600, the first flight of fighters would be launched. Throughout the day, other flights of fighters, dive bombers, torpedo planes, or photographic missions would take off and return until night fell. Later in the war, night fighters would continue throughout the dark.

The men of this floating city were part of a great adventure, but it was not all glory and glamour. They were continually reminded, but rarely mentioned, that death was a constant companion. Casualties on carriers were high and it made them value the gift of life. Experienced hands simply referred to the dark episodes as "incidents of service."

3.

Tarawa and Truk

The new carrier strike force meets its first challenge against the Japanese in the bloody operations at Tarawa and the air attack on the Japanese stronghold of Truk in the central Pacific.

Off the reef at Wake Island, the submarine *Skate* stood by. It was hardly a safe place to be and no one, least of all the enemy, would have known that she was on an errand of mercy. The Navy believed in taking care of her "lost lambs" and Commander McKinney's orders were to rescue any fallen pilots from the Fast Carrier Task Force. It was a noble idea, but *Skate* was having her own troubles. The first day, Japanese aircraft strafed the boat and seriously wounded one of her officers, Lieutenant (j.g.) W. E. Maxon. The next day, a coast defense gun spotted the submarine and forced her to submerge.

Sometime later, McKinney brought his boat up to the surface. He had received a message that three aviators were down and he started looking for them. The shellfire began again as the captain conned the boat toward the shore, risking himself and his crew, to pick up one flier from the water and another waiting in a rubber boat. McKinney held a law degree and there was a time when he had felt the need to prove himself to his men as a submariner. That time had passed. Now they knew he knew his business. Luckily, he missed the gunfire from shore, but during the search for the third aviator, an enemy dive bomber forced the submarine below again.

Meanwhile, Maxon's condition grew worse and McKinney headed for Midway. Then another message arrived that nine aviators were drifting off Wake. The decision that McKinney faced was enough to tear the heart out of any man. The life of his own officer was in jeopardy and yet the scales weighed nine against one. Worried as he was about Maxon, he could not ignore the plea. Reluctantly, he reversed course and found four of the aviators, but Maxon died of his wounds. The submariners had paid a high price for their courage. Still, they understood that rescue missions had become one more of their jobs.

Captain Stump, commanding officer of the new *Lexington*, dispatched a message to McKinney that gave some idea of the depth of airmen's sentiments. "Anything in *Lexington* is yours for the asking. If it is too big to carry away, we will cut it up in small parts!"

The strike on Wake was a time of testing. It was a preliminary for bigger things to come. The new air and sea power and new techniques had to be tried out. New pilots and crews needed combat experience, so "soft" targets were selected for flexing muscles and learning lessons.

Late in the summer of 1943, Rear Admiral Charles Pownall, an able aviator who had previously commanded the *Enterprise*, formed Task Force 15 and raised his flag in the *Yorktown*. The ship's name confused lots of people, mainly the Japanese. The old *Yorktown*, of course, had gone down at Midway. The new *Yorktown*, like the new *Lexington*, was another *Essex* class carrier.

In the force were the *Essex* and *Independence*, a light

carrier, and a screen of a fast battleship, two cruisers, and ten destroyers. Their first target was Marcus Island, a volcanic patch of one square mile, about fifteen hundred miles west of Midway. There Hellcats and Avengers, along with Dauntless SBDs, went to work on ground installations and enemy aircraft. Six strikes severely damaged almost everything in sight, but there was no such thing as a soft target. Three American fighters and one torpedo plane were lost.

Nevertheless, fast carriers were showing their ability to roam over the ocean and keep the enemy guessing. On the list of soft targets was Wake, where McKinney had waited. Twelve planes had been lost. It was an expensive exercise considered necessary for upcoming operations.

Less than three weeks later, Pownall joined a new *Lexington*, *Princeton*, and *Belleau Wood*, and struck hundreds of miles away at Tarawa and Makin in the Gilberts. The Japanese wondered where the Americans would strike next. Where would an invasion take place?

Preparations intensified for the assault on the Gilberts with Spruance in command. He was known as a man who ran a quiet bridge. No orders bellowed across the deck and his behavior was contagious. Everyone on the flag bridge seemed to speak in hushed tones. You could almost hear a pin drop. Part of Spruance's manner could be attributed to his natural disposition. He was a quiet man. Still, there must have been times, as the pressure grew, when it would have been much easier to let off steam. Ranting old sea dogs were legendary. But Spruance was a firm believer in discipline and self-restraint. His conduct was a matter of will as much as nature. Reason, not emotion, would win

36

battles, and he wanted cool heads. A graduate, and later member of the staff, of the Naval War College at Newport, he was an avid reader and looked upon war as an intellectual exercise. There was no room in his heart for hatred of the enemy.

Since Spruance was a strong man, his manner was never taken for weakness. Officers respected him and knew that

Admiral Raymond A. Spruance.

his dignity and tolerance could never be mistaken for indecision or lack of purpose. He did not have to set off fireworks so that everyone would know that he was commander in the central Pacific.

Still, with all of the gifts of mind and character, Spruance realized that he faced enormous challenges as he sailed in the cruiser *Indianapolis* toward the Gilbert Islands on the equator. It was the first major amphibious assault that aimed to improve communications, provide bases, and lead the way to the Marshalls, Carolines, and Marianas, ever closer to Japan. As overall commander of the operation called "Galvanic," Spruance had a powerful fleet that included the largest task force of fast carriers that the world had ever seen.

The carriers, under Pownall, were designated TF50, and consisted of six large carriers (CVs) and five light carriers (CVLs) formed into four task groups (TGs). The ships carried 700 aircraft. That was not all. The Fast Carrier Task Force had a screen of six fast battleships, three heavy cruisers, three antiaircraft cruisers, and twenty-one destroyers.

Despite this heavy concentration of air power, many airmen had grave misgivings about carriers operating so far from their own bases. Up to now the survival rate of carriers was not encouraging, and in the Solomons they had operated nearer to friendly airfields. To make matters worse, Spruance was not an aviator and that made airmen uneasy.

Another part of the fleet was the assault force under Rear Admiral R. K. Turner, a brilliant scrapper, who would land the 2nd Marine Division, veterans of Guadalcanal, on Tarawa, and the 27th Division of the United States Army on Makin. Eight small, slow escort carriers (CVEs), often called "baby" or "jeep" carriers, were in the amphibious forces and added 200 more aircraft. Their mission was to give direct support to the landings.

D-Day was November 20, 1943. Earlier in the month the fast carriers had split up on separate raiding assignments and hit the Marshalls, Gilberts, Bougainville, and Rabaul. The name "Rabaul" held special awe for Americans in the Pacific. It was a well-entrenched Japanese stronghold and this was the first carrier strike. Rabaul turned out to be a triumph for the F4U Corsair because the plane proved that it could operate effectively from a carrier.

The lightning raids took a heavy toll of enemy planes that far outnumbered American losses. Still, several United States planes were lost. At Rabaul, Commander Henry Caldwell flew his Avenger back to the *Saratoga* with a wounded gunner and a dead photographer. The plane had one wheel, no flaps, no aileron, and no radio. His escorting fighter took more than two hundred bullets and the pilot was hit but returned, too. Some seemed destined for hairbreadth escapes.

Now, as D-Day approached, the four task groups rendezvoused for the invasion of the Gilberts.

Intelligence officers pored over photographs from aerial and submarine reconnaissance of Tarawa and worried about the gaps in their information. Army Liberators as well as carrier planes had pounded the island, but their reports were confusing and some were worse than none. Liberator pilots, flying at 2,500 feet, reported no signs of life. Fortunately, skeptics took such reports with a grain of salt. They knew the island was heavily fortified, but it was hard to

39

spot targets under concrete, steel, and coconut logs. Other islands might have been easier to take, but Tarawa's airfield was the key. It was needed to support the next landings in the more strategically located Marshall Islands six hundred miles to the north.

Natural hazards were a threat too. At low tide the solid ring of sharp, jagged coral offshore could cause more grief than the man-made obstacles that blocked the beaches. The rocky, coral clusters could snag a landing boat and leave it high and dry.

Doubts were cast aside. The operation was on and it would have been reasonable to assume that the thousands of tons of shells and bombs dropped on the dot in the ocean had wiped the enemy off the face of the earth. The 2nd Marine Division found out differently.

On D-Day, Navy coxswains steered their landing boats toward the shore in their businesslike way while young Marines, many in their teens, joked with each other. But they did not fool themselves. They knew what the day might bring.

Suddenly, the routine landing turned into havoc. In high water the boats could have passed over the coral reef without trouble. Instead, the worst happened. An unexpected, abnormal tide hung many of the boats and tractors on the reef while murderous gunfire swept across them from shore. Private N. M. Baird, who landed in the first wave on Beach Red 1, said, "They were knockin' boats out left and right. A tractor'd get hit, stop, and burst into flames, with men jumping out like torches." He wondered why he was not hit too.

Some Marines waded through water up to their waists

for about three hundred yards before they reached the beach. As they clumsily worked their way forward, the withering fire continued. One Marine after another disappeared beneath the water or strewed the beach with their lifeless young bodies. Four tanks sank in potholes with their crews trapped inside. By the end of the first day five thousand men went ashore and about fifteen hundred of them were killed or wounded.

The Sasebo Seventh Special Landing Force under Commander Takeo Sugai and the Third Special Base Force were among the five thousand well-trained Japanese troops that held the island. Rear Admiral Keijo Shibasaki, the atoll commander, boasted that Tarawa could not be taken by a million men in a hundred years. On that first day there were times when it looked like he might have been right.

If the issue was in doubt in the beginning of the battle, and it was, there was no doubt at the end. In four days the Marines struggled against barbed wire barricades, strong defense guns, pillboxes, and a network of bombproof shelters. Aggressively and methodically they gained control of the island while the enemy fought to the death. Tarawa would become a name that would live in the history of the United States Marine Corps.

The landing at Makin the same day was another story. The 27th Division ran against light opposition from about eight hundred labor troops. However, Major General Holland M. Smith, a Marine known as "Howling Mad" Smith, commander of all ground forces, was not pleased with the slow-moving Army that took the same four days to secure the island. The Army way was not the Marine way. Bitter arguments broke out between the soldiers and the Marines

41

about the best tactics, and the bad feeling between the two services would linger for a long time to come.

Meanwhile, at sea, transports unloaded troops and equipment while warships bombarded the shore. Carrier planes strafed and bombed targets on the islands all day long, not always with the desired results. Thirty-two strikes were made on D-Day with eighty planes in one strike, and yet nothing seemed sufficient.

November 20 was a tough day for the Navy and the evening was worse. Dusk was always a dangerous time for the carriers. It brought out the enemy. Thirty miles west of Tarawa, sixteen Japanese torpedo bombers attacked Admiral Montgomery's fast carrier task group while they were recovering aircraft. Black bursts of antiaircraft fire filled the sky and failed to stop nine of the determined planes. Three headed for the *Essex* and *Bunker Hill* but did no damage. Six aimed for the *Independence*. Before five of the six were shot down, a torpedo rammed the light carrier and killed seventeen men and wounded forty-three others. Although the ship remained afloat, it had to leave the area for repairs.

On November 23, J. J. Clark, captain of the *Yorktown*, received word that five Wildcats from the *Liscome Bay* had lost their way and had come out of a storm near his ship. Clark, a part Cherokee Indian known as "Jocko," decided to take the strays aboard for the night. Two planes landed smoothly, the third did not. The plane bounced, hit the deck hard, and missed the arresting wire. The pilot neglected to lower his tail hook. Then he gunned the throttle by mistake, jumped over the wire barriers and crashed into the parked planes ahead.

Watching from the sidelines, Chief Boatswain's Mate John Montgomery knew what was going to happen next. Fire was a foregone conclusion. He shouted, "Get the foam started."

In the crash, the plane's belly tank exploded amid armed and fueled planes ready for takeoff the next morning. The pilot was thrown clear, but five deck crewmen died in the flames as ammunition and magnesium flares began to burn. The fire alarm blared away and the two remaining Wildcats circling above were told to land on the nearby *Lexington*.

Clark, witnessing the scene from the bridge, ordered his ship to steam into the wind in the hope that the other parked planes would not catch on fire. Then he saw the deck near the island structure grow white hot and the ammunition explode. He did not need much imagination to picture his ship a total wreck. The island would be the next to catch fire and all ship control would be lost. While he was thinking the worst, a man appeared in an asbestos suit and stood between the fire and the island. Clark's booming voice yelled directions from his vantage point while gasoline flowed down the deck and below into the hangar.

Montgomery took a fire nozzle and hose and walked under the planes into the fire, spraying foam everywhere. Lieutenant Bernard Lally, the ship's fire marshal, wearing protective gloves, joined him, and soon others joined the fight. Some of the men sprayed foam on Montgomery as he moved forward to get ahead of the fire. At any instant the flames could engulf him. Gasoline burned on top of the foam as it spread over the deck. It seemed like an eternity to the men of the *Yorktown*, and yet fourteen minutes later the fire was under control. Five blackened planes were dumped overboard and the ship was ready for action again. Clark made a mental note to have a few sharp words with the pilot the next day. He also intended to recommend the firefighters for the Navy and Marine Corps Medal.

That night, the little jeep carrier *Liscome Bay* stood off Makin preparing planes for early launching the next day. Clouds covered the moon, but it was a pleasant evening with a light breeze. Shortly before 0500, the cruiser *New Mexico* reported a surface radar contact which faded in a few minutes. Perhaps it was one more false contact. They happened all too frequently. Nevertheless, general quarters sounded on the *Liscome Bay* at 0505.

In the first light of day, Commander Tadashi Tabata, captain of the submarine I-175, prowled around offshore waters seeking a target. He found the *Liscome Bay*. At 0513, Tabata fired one or more torpedoes. One hit the CVE amidships and a tremendous explosion set off a bright flame that rose hundreds of feet into the air. The 2,000- and 1,000 pound bombs stored in the hold went off and the ship started to break up. Men and steel were thrown so high by the blast that parts of both came down on the *New Mexico*, fifteen hundred yards away. Fire rushed throughout the remains of the ship, more ammunition exploded, and the flight deck collapsed. The *Liscome Bay* was hell.

Captain John Crommelin, a member of Rear Admiral Mullinix's staff, was taking a shower when the torpedo hit. Stark naked, he ran out on deck, helped several men, suffered severe burns, and survived. Most were not so lucky.

Destroyers *Morris* and *Hughes*, among others, rushed to the scene to lend a hand. Their whaleboats were in the water in no time, and their seamen hauled everyone in sight into their boats. Survivors suffered horrible burns and wounds. Blistered and blackened men floundered in the fuel oil–covered sea. Blinded by the oil, many did not know that help was on the way. Rescue workers told of courageous men struggling in the water insisting that others be helped first. Heroism, unrecognized and unpublicized, was commonplace.

When the final count was made, 642 officers and enlisted men were gone. Among them were Admiral Mullinix, commander of TG52.3 Air Support Group, and I. D. Wiltsie, captain of the *Liscome Bay*. Most of the casualties were ordinary young men a long way from home who had wanted nothing more than peace and the opportunity to return home. In an instant their lives were snuffed out. The cost of Tarawa mounted.

On board the *Yorktown*, "Jocko" Clark had planned on having a few strong words with the unfortunate pilot from the *Liscome Bay*. The dejected young officer appeared before him on the bridge to apologize for the mishap the day before, but too much had happened for Clark to be angry. In a subdued mood, he simply said, "Well what you've done is incident to service. You'd better be glad you're here, because if you'd been on your own ship you might have gone down with her."

John Crommelin's brother, Charles, was a lieutenant commander leading an air group from the *Yorktown* against Mili in the Marshalls to the north that day. A shell hit his Hellcat and the explosion frosted the windshield, wrecked instruments, and blinded one of Crommelin's eyes and damaged the other. He could fly only by leaning out of the cockpit and looking into the slipstream with the better eye. He made the 120 miles back, landed on the *Yorktown*, taxied away from the arresting gear, parked the plane, climbed out, and collapsed.

One of the carriers off Makin making one strike after another was the "Big E." Her mission was to control the air over Makin, support landings, and stand by in case the Japanese Navy appeared on the horizon. Among the aviators on board was Lieutenant Commander Edward H. "Butch" O'Hare, who had become something of a legend. In 1942, off Bougainville, he ran into nine twin-engine Japanese bombers and shot down four in about five minutes. His performance saved the *Lexington* that day and won him the Congressional Medal of Honor, and his name appeared in newspapers across the United States. Almost all Americans had heard of "Butch" O'Hare. In the company of Navy men he was respected as a friendly, aggressive, and competent pilot.

O'Hare and some other officers on the *Enterprise* had developed an interest in the possibilities of night flying. Almost no combat operations were attempted in the dark for the simple reason that no one could see the enemy. The idea grew among these men that the ship's radar could locate a "bogey," an unidentified plane, and bring the pilot close enough so that an Avenger's radar could pick it up and carry on from there. But Avengers made poor fighters because they lacked speed, maneuverability, and gunpower. Hellcats would have to accompany them on each wing.

Off Makin, O'Hare took part in the experiment as a pilot of a Hellcat. The system worked when a Japanese Betty bomber was found on the scope and shot down. Afterward

46

something went wrong. Nobody knows what for sure. Still, it appears that a case of mistaken identity took place and the Avenger fired on O'Hare while he was moving to the right wing position. Whatever happened, O'Hare was never seen again. In time, night air combat based upon this and other pioneering efforts would be perfected. Again the cost was high. One of the great naval aviators of the war was lost, another incident of service.

In a few days, the operations in the Gilberts were over. It was a victory, but a tragic victory filled with sadness and the knowledge that there was still much to learn. No war was won. It was only a phase, one small step toward the Japanese homeland. Next on the list of landings was the Marshalls.

Fleet and task force commanders were apprehensive. Would the next assault be as costly as the last? How many such victories could the United States take? Commanders carefully studied the Gilberts experience to avoid future mistakes. Still, there were no guarantees in war, and no two experiences were exactly alike. Only time would tell as Spruance and Turner made plans for the next attack.

Much to Spruance's irritation, a new face appeared among his subordinate commanders for the Marshalls campaign. Admiral Nimitz had replaced Rear Admiral Pownall, the Fast Carrier Task Force commander, with Rear Admiral Marc Mitscher. Some of the air admirals undoubtedly had a hand in the change, but Spruance had respect for Pownall and hated to see him go. Their working relationship was good. Pownall cooperated with the "black shoe" Spruance and cooperation did not always come easily from "brown shoe" aviators.

Spruance and Mitscher were not well-acquainted personally. Nevertheless, they were known to each other professionally and each had doubts about the other. At the battle of Midway, Mitscher was captain of the *Hornet*, and Spruance was not especially pleased with his performance. After the battle, Spruance had questioned Mitscher's reports, which he considered inaccurate, and probably, if the truth were known, Mitscher was not too happy about the results himself.

After Midway, Mitscher was relegated to a dreaded shore assignment until Admiral Halsey rescued him and made him Commander, Air, Solomon Islands, a hot spot. Mitscher was a shrewd and effective air commander and Halsey's regard for him grew. Finally, worn out after months of strain, Mitscher had returned to another assignment in San Diego for a brief spell when he received the call to return to combat. The command did not come as a great compliment. He was an officer of rank and experience who just happened to be available at the time.

In many ways, Spruance and Mitscher were alike. In many ways, they were very different. Both men were shy and extremely quiet. Mitscher spoke so softly that "Jocko" Clark said he had to learn to read his lips. An officer on the *Saratoga* once said, "If you didn't hear him, you had better damn sight ask someone who did." Both men had unusual self-control, worked at standup desks, and surrounded themselves with a staff of the ablest officers they could find. Both men showed concern for those under them and in return received their respect.

The similarities between the two men could not be stretched too far. The small, wiry, wizened, bald-headed

Mitscher looked old beyond his years. His life had been spent outdoors and his weatherbeaten face showed it. As a boy he lived a life of riding, hunting, and fishing in untamed Oklahoma where his father was agent for the Osage Indian Reservation. At Annapolis, unlike Spruance, he was a poor student near the bottom of his class and he never attended the Naval War College at Newport. His career might have ended in mediocrity if he had not found a home in naval aviation.

Vice Admiral Marc A. Mitscher aboard the *Lexington*.

Mitscher was not a "Johnny-come-lately" to aviation like King, Halsey, and others who took up flying late in life to advance their careers. Mitscher reported for duty at Pensacola in 1915 and his first flight was in a flimsy wood, wire, and canvas plane with a 100-horsepower pusher engine. It was like flying a kite, and he loved it.

Four years later, Mitscher was a pilot of the NC-1, one of three Navy planes that attempted to fly across the Atlantic. Lost in the fog, the plane landed at sea and was unable to take off again. Hours passed before a Greek freighter saved them. The NC-3 also failed in the attempt, but the NC-4, commanded by Albert Read, succeeded in crossing the Atlantic via the Azores. It was eight years before Charles Lindbergh's solo flight from New York to Paris. Mitscher was a true air pioneer and if he needed a reason to be sympathetic toward downed fliers during the war he had a good one. He knew the empty feeling of being lost at sea with only a dim chance of rescue.

Through the peacetime years, Mitscher developed a reputation as a capable air officer. He had wide experience in a variety of aviation duties and he was known as a cautious pilot who did not take chances. After serving in the Bureau of Aeronautics, his chief, the hard taskmaster Admiral King, wrote that Mitscher was "a personality that inspires confidence and loyalty. Quiet, forceful, tactful, conscientous, steady, and practical. An asset to any organization." Those were rare words from a man like King. Nonetheless, Mitscher had to prove himself again.

Shortly before Mitscher arrived in the central Pacific, the fast carriers were reorganized again. Now they were known as Task Force 58. The numerical identification presented no special image. The first number indicated the fleet, and the second the force. Still, the potential power of TF58 was present, and like Mitscher, it had to prove itself. At the outset, TF58 consisted of twelve fast carriers and 700 aircraft. Mitscher became task force commander on January 29, 1944, and two days later the Marines landed at Kwajalein in the Marshalls.

The thirty-or-so islands of the Marshalls stretched out over an expanse of more than four hundred thousand square miles of ocean. Most of the coral atolls enclosed lagoons, and Kwajalein, the largest coral atoll in the world, had airfields and an anchorage. TF58 blasted the islands the same day that Mitscher assumed command. The lessons of Tarawa were applied with aggressive tactics that knocked out the enemy air power in the area. Two days later, the Marines landed on Kwajalein against heavy ground opposition but fortunately it was not a repetition of the bloody days at Tarawa. Another landing the same day at Majuro was unopposed and the commanders sighed with relief. The next day, Roi and Namur were occupied, and a few days later, amphibious forces landed at Eniwetok. All were islands in the Marshalls group.

With the amphibious operations well underway, Spruance decided to strike Truk, a bastion called the "Gibraltar of the Pacific." Mitscher left one of his task groups to support the Eniwetok landings and joined Spruance with the remaining three task groups of fast carriers.

For a long time it had been believed that Truk would have to be taken by an amphibious assault. It had been an island of mystery since shortly after World War I when the Japanese secretly began to build up the fortress. In 1942, it was the base for the Japanese Combined Fleet and hundreds of aircraft were known to be on its airfields. Now there was the possibility that the fast carriers could hit the stronghold hard and make it helpless and worthless. Truk would test the capability of the fast carriers.

Spruance would watch his new commander like a hawk. Normally, Spruance had complete confidence in the men under his command and gave them considerable freedom in handling their jobs. For now, Spruance held a tight rein on Mitscher. It was a time of probation.

Ninety miles off Truk, early in the morning of February 16, the carriers launched their attack. First off were the fighters from the *Bunker Hill, Enterprise, Essex, Intrepid,* and *Yorktown.* The plan was for the fighters to sweep the airfields and control the air. Enemy radar picked up the approaching planes, but their poor communications failed to spread the word to all the islands in the atoll. Some received the message, some did not.

Poor communications or not, enough enemy planes got off the ground in time to give plenty of trouble. Fifty fighters, Zekes, Rufes, Hamps, and Tojos, climbed to meet the attackers. Acrobatics filled the sky as fighters on both sides scrambled to gain an advantage. Twisting and turning, firing and being fired on, some succeeded and others failed. Planes blew up in the air, some dove straight downward to their end. The action was so fast and furious it was almost impossible to know exactly what was going on.

Lieutenant Commander William R. Kane, better known as "Killer" Kane, from the *Enterprise,* and his wingman Verne Ude found themselves with four Zekes attacking them from above. Quickly they maneuvered their Hellcats and

The carrier *Enterprise* with one of its planes overhead patrolling in the southwest Pacific. The *Saratoga* is in the background.

each pilot shot down one plane. Seconds later, another Zeke went after Ude. Again he was able to send a plane down in flames. Free to continue on their way, they strafed an airfield on Truk and Kane caught two Tojos that had just taken off. In five minutes Kane and Ude shot down five planes.

Lieutenant Jack Farley, with Ensign Linton Cox flying alongside, made a tight turn and obliterated a Rufe from behind. Then machine gun fire from a plane Farley never saw shot up his cockpit and wounded him in the leg and hand. Cox disappeared.

When the air cleared, it was obvious that despite losses, Navy pilots, resolute in their mission, had outmatched the enemy. That morning they destroyed thirty planes in the air and forty more on the ground. Back on board, one exhilarated pilot said, "These Grummans (Hellcats) are beautiful planes. If they could cook, I'd marry one."

This was only the beginning. After the fighters came the bombers. Eighteen Avengers struck the airfields with fragmentation and incendiary bombs. Eventually, more than a hundred planes were destroyed in the air and on the fields and an equal number were damaged. Ships caught in the harbor were also bombed and riddled. A light cruiser and four destroyers were sunk. Not every sortie was a success. Not every bomb was a hit. Bomb after bomb was a discouraging miss. The hits were always relatively few. The scrap was not a one-sided affair. The night of the seventeenth, a Japanese radar-equipped Kate torpedo plane sent one of her torpedoes into the *Intrepid* which was forced to retire with a jammed rudder, eleven dead, and seventeen wounded.

During the night, the *Enterprise* sent out the first night

carrier bomber attack. The sacrifices of O'Hare and others were starting to produce an effective system for night combat. Torpedo Ten's mission was to attack enemy shipping. Flying through the dark at an altitude of only 250 feet, half of the TBFs made direct hits, a far better average than the daylight raids. One TBF and crew failed to return and two others were damaged. The sacrifices continued, but night attacks now seemed practical. Round the clock bombing appeared to be a real possibility.

The next morning, TF58 continued the pursuit of the enemy. During the fray, Lieutenant George Blair, an *Essex* pilot, was shot down and ended up in the lagoon. The others saw him go down as the Japanese destroyer *Fumuzuki* sailed toward him. No one had any intention of leaving the pilot to the mercy of the enemy. Nine planes circled overhead to keep the destroyer away and a slow-moving Kingfisher floatplane from the *Baltimore* went in to rescue him under the nose of the enemy. Lieutenant (j.g.) D. F. Baxter, the Kingfisher pilot, arrived back on the *Baltimore* with Blair and one pint of gasoline in his tank. Baxter had nerve. He had intentionally left that morning short of fuel so that he could carry the weight of another man.

The smashing of Truk proved that the fast carrier tactics were working. In the past month they had ranged over the seas creating havoc and only the *Intrepid* had been damaged.

Mitscher had every reason to be satisfied with recent events, but his silent behavior remained the same. A day or two after the success at Truk, an aide noticed Mitscher sitting in his swivel chair on the bridge at sunset in a pensive, contented mood. The officer asked the admiral what he was thinking about and expected a weighty answer. Mitscher replied, "I was just thinking at home the trout season opens today."

Spruance was obviously impressed by Mitscher's cool command of the task force. If he did not say so, he showed his feelings by sending Mitscher alone to strike the Marianas.

Confidence grew in carrier power and mobility. Seamen and airmen looked to the future with new hope. TF58 was beginning to mean more than a number to the men in the Pacific. The strike on Truk was a revolution in naval warfare. Now the aircraft carrier was the capital ship that counted. Its potential was unlimited.

4.

Battle of the Philippine Sea

Aircraft of the Japanese Mobile Fleet clash in a
head-on air battle off the Marianas with planes
from the fast carriers of Task Force 58.

Ferdinand Magellan, sailing across uncharted seas, had
discovered the Marianas in 1521 when he attempted to circle
the globe. The great navigator called them "Thieves Islands."
Centuries later, Japan took over all except one of the islands.
The one island they did not control was Guam, which had
become a United States possession. At the outset of World
War II, Japan took care of the exception by successfully
invading Guam. Now she had a total grip on the five-
hundred-mile volcanic chain, fifteen hundred miles east of
the Philippines.

To the sharp mind of Admiral King, the Marianas were
the key to conquest in the western Pacific. A look at a map
gives a good clue to his thoughts. From the mainland of
Japan, the north-south string of the Bonin Islands and the
Marianas were a direct pathway to and from the Japanese
far-flung bases in the Carolines and Bismarck Archipelago.
They were also a protective barrier for the Philippines and
Southeast Asia which were economically essential for the
health of the Empire.

The Japanese High Command shared Admiral King's
views about the Marianas. They realized that their loss
would lead to final defeat and instituted a "Z" plan for their
defense. The plan envisioned luring the United States Navy

57

into striking distance of their fleet and then attacking with land-based as well as carrier aircraft. The Marianas, they believed, would serve them well as "unsinkable carriers."

The Japanese had suffered severe blows in the past few months. Both battles and leaders had been lost. The highly respected Admiral Isoroku Yamamoto, Commander-in-Chief of the Combined Fleet, had been intercepted and shot down in the air. His successor, Admiral Mineichi Koga, was lost in a storm while flying from Palau to Davao in a four-engine seaplane.

Despite setbacks, careful planning and luck could save the day. Admiral Soemu Toyoda, the new commander-in-chief, gathered his forces for the inevitable showdown. He revised the "Z" plan into an "A" plan which organized all of the major surface ships into a single striking force under the astute Vice Admiral Jisaburo Ozawa. It was called the Mobile Fleet. Nine carriers were still afloat, and the improved Zeke, new Judy dive bomber, and the new Jill torpedo plane made their timely appearance to add extra power. (As the war went on, the Americans had given the enemy fighters male names and the bombers female names for easy identification.) The speedy Zeke could now reach 358 miles per hour and the Judy was not far behind, but they would still have to reckon with the American Hellcats. At Tawi Tawi in the Sulu Archipelago of the southern Philippines, the Japanese fleet was ready for any threat from the east near the Marianas or from the south near Hollandia, New Guinea.

After the strike on Truk, TF58 seemed to be everywhere. Mitscher, now a vice admiral, directed his men and ships with deceptive ease as they swiftly steamed from one target to another. Still silent, he spent most of his days sitting in

58

his high swivel chair on the *Yorktown* flag bridge facing aft with his feet against the base of the compass. Hour after hour, he quietly studied dispatches, watched the activities astern, and whispered his orders from his lofty perch. One of the much-discussed mysteries on the flagship was why Mitscher faced aft. It seemed like strange behavior and became a favorite conversation piece among the men as various theories developed. Could he hear talk in flag plot better while sitting in that direction? Was his ear closer to the porthole? Was he more interested in the action on the stern of the ship? There was really no mystery. He just wanted to avoid the wind on his already weatherbeaten face.

Sometimes Mitscher left his favorite spot and walked into flag plot to look at charts, work at his standup desk, or sit down on the leather sofa and ask his staff officers questions and listen to what was on their minds.

The greater mystery might have been why this wispy little man was turning into an outstanding war leader. Never flamboyant, he did not make the slightest effort to project a dramatic personality. And yet, the signals were clear. His men learned that he was an aggressive fighter, he knew his business, and his concern for his subordinates was genuine. Like all champions, he simply made the difficult look easy. His remarkable composure, except for smoking entirely too many cigarettes, hid the strain, worry, and heavy thinking that he exerted every day in trying to crush the enemy. Later, he was aptly called a "nautical Jeb Stuart" who, like the Confederate cavalry officer, dashed from behind weather fronts to make his attacks.

Still, Mitscher was no superman. At times he showed human failings like ordinary people. In March, in accordance with a new policy set by Admiral King, air admirals were required to have a nonaviator chief of staff, and the reverse was true as well. Nonair admirals, such as Spruance, were forced to accept an airman for chief of staff. Theoretically, it was a sound idea that aimed at combining the thoughts of men of different training and background. Practically, neither Spruance nor Mitscher had the least desire to make the change, but Mitscher went to extremes to express his displeasure.

Mitscher's new chief of staff was a relatively young officer well-known to Navy men throughout the Pacific. He was Captain Arleigh Burke, commander of a destroyer division, known as "31 Knot" Burke for his fast speeds and daring feats in the Solomons. Burke was happy with destroyers, but presumably the new billet would broaden his experience.

Mitscher had little interest in breaking in the new man. Irritated and unimpressed by this hero of the Solomons, the diehard aviator did his best to ignore his nonaviator staff member who had been foisted upon him. He overlooked, bypassed, and generally gave Burke the cold shoulder. Perhaps Mitscher thought he was testing the newcomer to determine the depth of his character. Or perhaps he did not care to have a colorful officer like Burke on his staff. Whatever his reasons, his behavior toward Burke was shortsighted and hardly cricket.

Burke, miserable and uncomfortable in this new setting, learned as much as he could about fast carriers without help from Mitscher. In time, when he believed he was right, sparks flew between the two men, and Burke held his ground. Slowly, Mitscher recognized the talents of this officer even if he did not know how to fly an airplane.

Gradually, they became acquainted, the freeze melted, and Burke became a valued and accepted member of the team. Years later, Burke would become the Chief of Naval Operations.

By now, Mitscher's favorite, "Jocko" Clark, was a rear admiral in command of one of the task groups. The task force commander liked Clark's rough fighting style and always placed him near the enemy. Clark's group was first in and last out of any operation. The other group commanders had also sharpened their aggressive tendencies to fit the Mitscher pattern. At the moment, they were Alfred Montgomery, Jack Reeves, and Ted Sherman. Each had his own eccentricities and jealousies that often led to scraps among themselves, but Mitscher knew how to keep them in line. His piercing blue eyes spoke far more volumes than his words and quickly told a man where he stood. And there was no question that when a man failed to measure up he did not stay around TF58 very long. .

Mitscher hit the Palau Islands in the Carolines in March and added a new twist. For the first time, aerial mines were dropped by carrier planes to block the main harbor. His one disappointment was that he had barely missed the Japanese fleet which had recently departed for a safer haven. Nevertheless, there was plenty to do. In April, he spent four profitable days raiding bases in New Guinea and creating general havoc.

Toward the end of April, Truk showed signs of reviving from its earlier drubbing. Ninety Japanese fighters had recently startled Army Liberator pilots by attacking them as they approached the island on what they thought would be something of a "milk run." It was obvious that the Navy

61

would have to tackle Truk again with its precision bombing. The Army Air Force believed in flying at high altitudes and the results were just not as effective.

TF58 set out with twelve carriers to shut down Truk once and for all. The *Yorktown* Plan of the Day read, "Today we start a two day return engagement at that popular theater which was so receptive on our last visit. This time we intend our performance to knock them completely off their feet."

Dispatches and messages from commanders frequently included such lighthearted attempts to amuse the men. The humor was often strained, the literary quality lacking, and few passages would ever compete with the pronouncements of John Paul Jones. Yet, this kind of trivia spread throughout the ships and created good-natured talk in the task force and made the day a little easier. Sometimes it took surprisingly little to break the tension or the boredom.

The second strike on Truk was not without problems. The men on the dying island fortress fought with every ounce of their waning power. A Zeke attacked Robert Kranze, a lieutenant (j.g.) flying a TBF on a photographic mission. He bailed out and others watched him float downward, but it was too late in the day to rescue him. Through the long night he sat in his little one-man raft near the reef wondering about his fate.

Kranze was not forgotten. The next day, Bombing and Torpedo 10 made a run on their island targets and then ignored clouds of antiaircraft fire to search for the missing man. They spotted him, passed the word, and soon two Kingfishers from the *Enterprise* appeared on the scene with four fighters protecting them. One of the slow floatplanes landed on the choppy water. Kranze latched onto the nearest float and the delicate plane capsized and dumped its two fliers into the sea.

The second plane came down. Two men in the water carefully climbed up each on a wing to balance the plane and the third took a position near the fuselage. There was only one trouble. The load was too heavy for takeoff so the pilot, Lieutenant (j.g.) John Burns, taxied to meet the submarine *Tang* which took the survivors aboard.

Burns was not finished. Flying around the east side of the atoll, he found another pilot waiting to be rescued. He landed again while a Hellcat circled overhead. Burns picked up his man and then tried to take off in the rough water. Again, it was no use. The conditions were impossible. Burns talked to another pilot on the radio about his unpleasant plight and the second pilot relayed the situation to the *Tang*. Dick O'Kane, captain of the *Tang*, answered that he would meet Burns but it would take him three hours to arrive.

Burns waited, and while waiting taxied around the ocean and picked up six more anxious, exhausted fliers from Torpedo 10. Practically tiptoeing onto the plane to prevent capsizing, seven men spread out on the wings as Burns slowly taxied to his rendezvous with *Tang*. By 1700 hours, all nine men were on board the submarine and the noble Kingfisher, its mission more than accomplished, was sunk with machine gun fire by the *Tang's* crew. The *Tang* had a profitable day too. The boat had rescued twenty-two men. The irony would be that O'Kane and some of his surviving crew would eventually end up in a Japanese prison camp. But O'Kane also received the Congressional Medal of Honor as the top submarine ace of the war.

The second strike on Truk, added to the other string of

successful raids, made an impressive list as the Fifth Fleet planned the invasion of Saipan, the largest island in the Marianas. Initially, there had been some opposition and lack of interest in the plan. Now, King had the support of the Army Air Force which had a new superfortress, the B-29. The Marianas, the Air Force realized, would make an excellent base for long-range raids on the Japanese mainland.

From King on down, the Navy eagerly looked forward to the Marianas. They hoped and believed that it would be more than an invasion. It was the time and place to face the Japanese fleet in an air and surface action. The Fifth Fleet was in tip-top shape, its power was unrivaled, and its commander was confident. Yet Spruance had specific orders. His primary purpose was to protect the landing on Saipan.

Spruance in the cruiser *Indianapolis* and Mitscher in the *Lexington* headed for battle. The Fifth Fleet was an armada of more than six hundred ships. TF58 alone consisted of seven heavy and eight light fast carriers, seven fast battleships, three heavy and seven light cruisers, and a mighty array of sixty destroyers. Packed on the fast carriers was the striking force of 448 Hellcat day fighters, twenty-seven Hellcat and Corsair night fighters, 174 Helldiver bombers, fifty-nine Dauntless bombers, and 193 Avenger torpedo bombers.

Seven old battleships, six heavy and five light cruisers, and more destroyers protected the transports, cargo ships, and landing craft of Turner's Fifth Amphibious Force. And under the surface there were twenty-eight submarines silently searching for prey.

As the ships sailed westward, solid information was crucial. Still, with all of their power, technology, and mobility, good information was surprisingly scarce. Radio transmissions from submarines and air patrols were erratic and frustrating. Spruance received pieces of information, but never a complete picture.

TF58 left the Majuro anchorage in the Marshals on June 6, a momentous day for all Americans in another part of the world where another invasion took place on the beaches of Normandy. All hands eagerly listened to radio reports about the European theater while they looked forward with anticipation to their own D-Day on June 15.

For four days prior to the landing of the 2nd and 4th Marine Divisions, carrier aircraft swept through Guam, Saipan, and Tinian, and as far north as Iwo Jima, and destroyed dozens of land-based planes.

Although protection of the landing was uppermost in Spruance's mind, thoughts of a possible encounter with the enemy fleet were ever present. The troubling question was: where was the Japanese fleet? Reports continued to give only vague indications. The lack of clarity was maddening, but there was every reason to believe that the enemy fleet was on the way. On D-Day, June 15, the submarine *Flying Fish* sighted the Japanese entering the Philippine Sea.

Ozawa, confident of victory, or at least giving the impression of confidence, had sailed through the Philippine Islands and into the Philippine Sea via San Bernardino Strait. Tense with expectation, Ozawa rallied his men with the same message that Admiral Togo had delivered to the fleet before the victorious battle of Tsushima in the Russo-Japanese War. "The fate of the Empire," he said, "rests on this one battle. Every man is expected to do his most."

On June 16, Ozawa gave orders to commence Operation A. That same day his fleet was strengthened by the arrival of Vice Admiral Matome Ugaki's task force of two battle-ships, two heavy cruisers, one light cruiser, and five destroyers.

Weighing the might of each side, it was clear that the Japanese were outnumbered. And yet, they had certain advantages. Since their planes had neither armor nor self-sealing gas tanks, their search and attack range was greater. Their land-based planes were nearby and played a big part in their optimistic plans. Equally important, their carrier planes did not have to worry about returning to their ships if they ran low on fuel. The airfields of the Marianas were at their disposal. Finally, the easterly trade winds favored the Japanese. The American carriers would have to sail away from the enemy into the wind each time they launched their planes. The Japanese could launch and recover their planes while approaching the enemy. Time and distance were on the side of the Imperial Japanese Navy.

As Ozawa moved closer, the American landings on Saipan proceeded in an orderly manner. There was plenty of resistance, but the situation was under control.

The shrewd Japanese commander decided to strike at his maximum range of about four hundred miles. That was beyond the effective range of American planes and would give him a margin of safety. With battleships in the van he moved relentlessly forward.

Spruance planned to place his heavy ships in the van too so that the carriers would be protected. If the enemy appeared, both sides would seek to knock out the carriers. Still, Spruance did not know from which direction the enemy would appear, especially since the Japanese traditionally split their forces.

On the eighteenth, American search planes sighted the Japanese search planes, but not the fleet. Late that night, radio direction finding equipment monitored messages from Ozawa to the air force on the Marianas. On that basis, which was speculative and uncertain, the enemy was about three hundred fifty miles west of TF58.

Mitscher studied every scrap of information as eagerly as Spruance did. He proposed to Spruance that he close with the Japanese to the west so that he could launch his planes at the earliest possible time in the morning to catch the fleet. Spruance, under enormous pressure, had confusing submarine reports that indicated the Japanese might be approaching in two separate groups. No one knew for sure. He would have preferred to steam westward too, but he turned down Mitscher's request and emphasized the possibility of an "end run." He had good reason to fear that one group of enemy ships might serve as a decoy while another hit the amphibious ships. The Japanese loved such tactics and Spruance was keenly aware of his first responsibility to defend the Saipan beachhead. It also crossed his mind that Admiral Togo had waited at Tsushima Strait for the Imperial Russian Fleet to come to him. He did not want to be trapped in the same way.

Air officers were aghast over Spruance's decision. They saw this as a lost opportunity to strike the first blow and destroy the enemy fleet. Mitscher said little and retired to his cabin.

The next day a Navy PBM flying boat made contact with the Japanese Fleet. Forty ships in two groups appeared on the screen. The pilot sent off a message about his find, but communication difficulties diluted its value. Some units failed to relay the message and the critical report was lost for seven-and-a-half hours.

TF58 sent out search planes regularly and fanned out as far as 325 miles without success. Some, unknown to themselves, were only forty or fifty miles away from the Japanese lead ships. At 0530 on the nineteenth, Spruance had still not received the report from the PBM. Nevertheless, the day of battle had begun. About that time, radar picked up two enemy planes approaching from the east. A Hellcat from the *Monterey* found the two Judy dive bombers and shot down one. Minutes later, five or six Zekes, probably from Guam, hovered over TF58 but did no harm. A destroyer shot down one and the others ran off.

More radar reports appeared and the air activity increased. Thirty-three Hellcats from the *Belleau Wood*, *Cabot*, *Hornet*, and *Yorktown* spent a busy two hours in hectic dogfights over Guam. At a cost of one Hellcat, they destroyed thirty fighters and five bombers. Just as more Japanese planes took off to meet them, the Hellcats received word to break off action and return to their ships. Bigger things were brewing. The message to bring the pilots back was the old circus yell, "Hey Rube," that had been used by carriers since 1942.

Radar had picked up a raft of "bogeys" approaching from the west. The waiting was over. The main attack had begun. At 1030, TF58 turned into the wind and launched its fighters.

The cool, deliberate Ozawa had started to work early. Long before sunrise, he had his search planes scanning the seas for the enemy carriers. By 0830 he had the search reports that he had waited for and ordered the first strike from *Chitose*, *Chiyoda*, and *Zuiho*. Sixty-one Zeros and eight Jill torpedo bombers were in the air. Less than a half-hour later, a second strike roared into the sky with forty-eight Zeros and twenty-seven Jills from the *Shokaku, Taiho,* and *Zuikaku.*

Warrant Officer Sakio Komatsu, a dedicated pilot, noticed a torpedo on its inexorable way toward his ship, the huge *Taiho,* almost immediately after he had taken off. Without a second thought, he dove into the torpedo and exploded it only a hundred yards away from the target. As Ozawa and others on the *Taiho* watched Komatsu's self-sacrifice, a second torpedo hit the starboard side. It appeared to do little damage as the rugged carrier sailed on.

The torpedoes had come from the submarine *Albacore,* commanded by James Blanchard. He had found himself, as he patrolled in his assigned area, in the middle of Ozawa's carriers and took aim to fire a salvo at *Taiho.* At the decisive moment the torpedo-firing computer failed. Blanchard cursed his luck and quickly made his own estimate at a range of about five thousand yards. It was a tricky business since the carrier was making a speedy twenty-seven knots, but he let go with six torpedoes from the bow tubes.

Three or more destroyers rapidly pursued the *Albacore* as it dove deep. Blanchard heard two torpedo explosions amid the sounds of depth charges coming uncomfortably close. At least, he thought, he had the satisfaction of two hits on a carrier.

At 1000, Mitscher's radar picked up the approach of Ozawa's first strike and within ten minutes ordered every available fighter into the air. Pilots rushed to their planes and soon took off the deck in wild patterns that only they understood.

A Japanese fighter takes off from a Japanese aircraft carrier.

Controllers on board ship directed the Hellcats to the fray. Soon the air waves were filled with frantic messages from controllers to pilots, and pilots to pilots. "Vector two two five." "Tallyho, Tallyho." "Lookout, Jack. You've got one on your tail."

Lieutenant (j.g.) Stanley Vraciu, an ace with twelve kills in the air to his credit, was an unhappy Hellcat pilot that morning. Nothing seemed to go right. His engine threw oil and he could not keep up with his squadron commander. Five other fighters lagged behind too and the controller ordered them to stay clear of the action. Vraciu's supercharger acted up and the fighter director told him to orbit near the *Lexington*. He checked his instruments as he orbited and found that the engine gauges were normal and the slow-moving engine was running smoothly. He circled and circled for twenty-five minutes. Then, abruptly, the fighter director ordered, "Vector two six five."

Vraciu and the other five stragglers banked into a 265-degree heading. About twenty-five miles west of the *Lexington*, Vraciu sighted three unidentified planes about ten miles away. "Tallyho," he shouted. As they closed on the enemy, the three dots in the air multiplied. He thought there must have been fifty. He called again, "Tallyho, eleven o'clock low." Other Hellcats joined them.

The enemy planes, Zekes, Judys, and Jills, were at about seventeen thousand feet. Each Hellcat sighted a target. Despite obstructed vision from his oil-smeared canopy, Vraciu spotted a Judy. He squeezed his trigger and the Judy broke into bits. He steered clear of the wreckage and yelled, "Splash one Judy."

In another instant he was behind two Judys flying side by

71

side. With the throttle all the way forward, Vraciu sped toward them, fired his six guns, and took out one and then the other.

The enemy planes were after the carriers, but most of them failed to penetrate that far. One bombed the *South Dakota*, doing little harm to the battleship but killing twenty-seven men. Another crashed into the *Indiana* without any effect on that tough battleship.

The battle continued hot and heavy. In the tangle, Vraciu shot down a third attacker and then radioed the *Lexington*, "Don't see how we can possibly shoot 'em all down. Too many." Nonetheless, he kept on going and dived toward a fourth Judy. Again he closed from the rear. Again an enemy plane splashed.

Next, Vraciu went after a Judy making a dive-bombing run on a ship and almost got caught in the antiaircraft fire himself, but he scored his fifth victim, and in another minute his sixth. Six planes down in six minutes.

Other pilots were running up scores too. Their excellent training was paying off. The air cleared and the enemy had taken a terrible beating. Commander David McCampbell's VF15 from the *Essex* had destroyed sixty. planes. The *Lexington's* VF16 downed forty-four and lost four. The slow-starting Vraciu's individual score was the high for the squadron, but Ensign Wilbur Well of the *Hornet* tied him.

On the way back to the *Lexington*, Vraciu was almost shot down by friendly antiaircraft fire. He took a detour, thinking unkind thoughts, and landed safely. As he taxied to the parking area, he looked up at the bridge and noticed Mitscher looking down with a grin on his face. The admiral greeted the pilot, shook his hand, and then stepped aside for the pilot to hold the limelight. A little later, Mitscher shyly asked to pose with the young hero. "Not for publication;" he said, "to keep for myself."

The morning was not over. At 1107, TF58 radar announced the appearance of Ozawa's second raid. Hellcats went to work again. More than a hundred Japanese planes attacked and only a handful reached the carriers. A bomb exploded over the *Wasp* and killed one man and wounded a dozen others. Near-misses on the *Bunker Hill* killed three men and wounded seventy-three. Some Jill torpedo planes got through to the carriers and then failed to do any damage. Most Japanese planes were shot down in dogfights and their losses were staggering. Only about fifteen planes from the Japanese second strike survived.

Nevertheless, the third strike of forty Zeros and seven Jills from the *Hiyo, Junyo,* and *Ryuho* were on the way. Their record was equally dismal. They inflicted no damage and many returned to their carriers without finding a target. Still a fourth raid of eighty-two planes failed miserably and decided to land on Rota and Guam. At Guam, Hellcats from the *Cowpens, Essex,* and *Hornet* greeted the Japanese over their own islands. Seventy-three of the eighty-two planes never flew again.

By three o'clock in the afternoon there were reasons galore for the Navy pilots to be proud of their day's work. The tally showed incredible enemy losses of more than three hundred aircraft. The Americans lost twenty-three planes in combat and six in accidents. Twenty pilots and seven air crewmen were lost plus thirty-one men aboard the fast carriers. One pilot called the day's activities a "Turkey Shoot" and the name stuck. The phrase had a cruel ring, but they played a cruel game that day.

The great Japanese deficiency was not aircraft. It was lack of well-trained, experienced pilots.

The loss of one pilot upset Mitscher and he never reported "only" one lost as some commanders did. Usually, he wrote "unfortunately." Their deaths sickened him. He fretted over his men and his love for them was only matched by his loathing for the enemy. Unlike Spruance, he hated the Japanese with a vengeance.

Meanwhile, the one torpedo hit on the *Taiho* magnified in importance. Gasoline fumes spread throughout the ship without the crew's awareness. About 1530, the volatile fumes ignited like a keg of dynamite. The flight deck erupted, and the sides of the ship blew out. The end was near for the newest and largest carrier in the fleet.

Admiral Ozawa preferred to go down with the ship, but the staff persuaded him to transfer to the cruiser *Haguro*. Captain Toshikazu Ohmae, his senior staff officer, said, "The battle is still going on and you should remain in command for the final victory." Shortly after Ozawa departed, a second explosion completed the destruction and the ship disappeared stern first with 1,650 officers and men. Weeks passed before Blanchard, captain of the *Albacore*, learned the news of his devastation.

That same afternoon, big, affable Herman Kossler, captain of the submarine *Cavalla*, found the heavy carrier *Shokaku* in his periscope. *Shokaku*, a victorious participant at Pearl Harbor, was on every Navy man's wanted list.

Kossler moved in and fired six torpedoes at a range of

about one thousand yards. Then in seconds, he took his boat down. He figured from the distinctive sounds that he heard as he submerged that he made three hits. Actually, he did better. Four torpedoes hit *Shokaku*. The hangar flooded, the bow settled, and she sank into the sea. The prize was not without a penalty. For the next three hours over a hundred depth charges dropped around the submarine and gave the crew of the *Cavalla* some nervous moments. Nevertheless, after their long ordeal they escaped without a scratch.

By 1500, Spruance knew that the Japanese air strikes had been a failure and signaled the restless Mitscher to go after the enemy fleet. After five long hours, the twelve carriers of three task groups recovered the hundreds of scattered planes and sailed west.

The next day, United States search planes stretched their range to 325 miles and still could not find the target they sought. The Japanese Mobile Fleet wisely remained just beyond their limit. Desperately anxious to find the carriers, twelve Hellcats flew the longest carrier search of the war without luck. They flew 475 miles, but the enemy was not in their sector.

Ozawa had transferred his flagship once more to the *Zuikaku* to gain better communications. Reports flowed in from his pilots that must have improved the admiral's spirits and set a new record for inaccuracy. From their accounts he had sunk or damaged four or five carriers, and one battleship or cruiser. With such a favorable count, he planned to continue the battle the next day.

At 1540 on the twentieth, Lieutenant Robert S. Nelson, flying an Avenger from the *Enterprise*, finally sighted the Japanese fleet. Mitscher received Nelson's report minutes

75

later. It was badly garbled in transmission but said enough for Mitscher. The time of day was late and he had to make a decision. The sun would set in three hours. Could he attack and still recover his planes? It would be dark and the cost was bound to be high. Would his planes be effective for combat after flying their maximum range? He did not take long to make up his mind. At 1610, the order went out for every available plane to strike.

Ten minutes later, pilots manned their aircraft. Eighty-five fighters, seventy-seven dive bombers, and fifty-four torpedo planes were in the air while a second strike group got set. Chalked on blackboards in ready rooms was the phrase, "Get the carriers."

The burden for the dangerous decision was on Mitscher. All he could do now was wait. High losses could turn victory into a catastrophe and he was keenly aware of all the negatives. He knew that his pilots were tired and that he was demanding their utmost. The rewards could be great but there were bound to be casualties. He knew better than anyone that daylight-trained pilots would be lost at night. Recovery would be slow work. He thought it would take four hours.

After the first strike had taken off, Mitscher learned that the Japanese fleet was sixty miles farther away than first estimated. The distance from the enemy was further increased by his carriers continually sailing eastward away from them to launch planes. The fighters and dive bombers had been fitted with drop tanks for a maximum range of about two hundred twenty miles. Now, the distance was more like three hundred miles. When Mitscher received the revised information, he canceled the second strike. The first strike continued on into the unknown.

The pilots sighted Japanese ships at 1840 as the sun sank lower and lower in the west. They saw oilers and destroyers when they wanted to see carriers. Thirty-five more miles west, the battleships, cruisers, and destroyers screening Carrier Division 3 appeared. A few more miles to the north were Carrier Divisions 1 and 2.

The Hellcats could not waste time. Fuel was too precious. They made a beeline for sixteen planes circling to land on the carriers. Seven were shot down, but the seven carriers were able to launch about seventy-five planes, most of them Zeros. Antiaircraft fire came in all colors as the Hellcats attacked. The blue, yellow, lavender, pink, red, white, and black puffs were all equally deadly signs. The golden sunset added to the hue and created a peaceful setting for a ghastly encounter.

In the next twenty minutes, Hellcats, Helldivers, and Avengers ferociously dived, strafed, bombed, and torpedoed in their anxiety to finish the carriers and start back.

Lieutenant (j.g.) George Brown, determined to get a carrier, went after the *Hiyo*. Part of his left wing was shot away, flames broke out, and the radioman and gunner jumped. Brown kept on going, dropped a torpedo, and started to return. On the way back two other planes tried to keep in contact with him because it was obvious that he was wounded and could not control his plane. Passing through a cloud he disappeared forever. Other Avengers fired two torpedoes into the *Hiyo* and it was a goner.

Two bombs dropped on the *Junyo* and six near-misses

77

caused some damage and slowed her air activity. It did not sink the ship.

The *Ryuho* remained unscathed while the *Zuikaku* took a number of damaging near-misses and at least one direct bomb hit. It looked like the end for the big ship. Fires flared up and the order was given to abandon ship. However, the frantic Japanese found in a short time that they could control the fire and rescinded the order.

The American pilots thought they had sunk two carriers, which was a sensible assumption since the Japanese had thought that the *Zuikaku* was finished. In the final tally, *Hiyo* was sunk, *Zuikaku* and two oilers were severely damaged, and a number of ships received minor damage. It was not an impressive score, but in the dwindling light it was probably the best that could be expected. Most of the Avengers carried bombs and in retrospect they probably would have done better with torpedoes. In the air duels, however, the Japanese were utterly routed. Sixty-five of their carrier planes were destroyed.

Whatever the score, the exhausted attackers now had the task of returning to their carriers and landing safely. Fighter pilots, alone with their thoughts, certainly must have had their share of doubts as they tried to conserve their remaining fuel. No one would ever know the thousands of stray notions, good and bad, that crossed their minds as their engines droned on. They did not even know exactly where they would find the carriers which had been steaming to close the gap by sailing westward. In the dark sky, all formations were forgotten. Planes flew back singly, in pairs, and in haphazard groups. Some decided to ditch together if they had to so that rescuers could spot them more easily.

The spectacular glow of the evening sunset had turned into a very dark night. The sky was overcast and there was a long way to go. Some ran out of fuel faster than others and ditched far from the carriers. Others reached the carriers and then ran out of fuel waiting their turn to land.

Mitscher spread his force over a fifteen-mile area to give room for the recovery. By 2045 the returning planes started to circle. The task force turned to the east and the recovery began. Mitscher gave an order that would be talked about for months in the Pacific. He disregarded enemy submarines and possible aircraft and told the ships under his command to turn on their lights. Others had done the same thing, but never under such dramatic circumstances. Every possible light shined brightly, truck lights, deck lights, running lights, and signal lights. Starshells shot through five-inch guns gave the night a carnival look.

But it was not a carnival. Pilots suffering from fatigue paid no attention to flight patterns. Planes circling to land crowded each other. Some, unaccustomed to night flying, were blinded or confused by the lights. Landing intervals were forgotten and planes crashed on deck. Others, angry and tired, refused to obey the signals of the landing signal officer. They simply could not wait any longer. The five strenuous hours in the air had built up too much tension. An Avenger, warned off by an LSO, proceeded to land, knocked a wing off, crashed into a Helldiver, and killed two men. Deck crews pushed aircraft overboard to make room for others.

Some who ditched into the sea were picked up within ten minutes. Some were never seen again. Joseph Kane, a Helldiver pilot from Bombing 14, landed in the water, grabbed his raft, and helped his gunner out of the rear. They drifted for the next five hours. Sick to his stomach, Kane spent his time with "dry heaves." Their situation seemed hopeless when three carriers and a cruiser passed them by unseen. Finally, the destroyer *Bell* fished them out of the water.

About half of the aircraft landed on the wrong carriers. No one had the slightest objection, any port in a storm. One pilot was flabbergasted to learn that he had landed on his own carrier. It was certainly not by design.

The dead-tired pilots who returned safely felt a sense of relief, but not a sense of glory. The ordeal had almost exceeded their endurance. Some were utterly disgusted. One said he had a bellyfull of war, and another claimed that he would never fly again. Others expressed similar statements. And yet they did fly again.

By the twenty-second, hope had faded for the well-known veteran of many battles, Commander "Killer" Kane. Then far in the distance, a destroyer approached the *Enterprise* and signaled, "How much ice cream is 'Killer' Kane worth?" The *Enterprise*, quite willing to pay any blackmail, received the aviator with a boisterous welcome. As the pilot came over in a breeches buoy it was obvious that he was not looking his best. Black eyes and a bandaged head did not help his appearance, but he was safe.

A long time later, the men of the *Enterprise* would have another surprise. Lieutenant William Faye went down in the Philippines and guerrillas protected him for three-and-a-half months. Finally, a PBY seaplane picked him up. When his air group returned to Pearl Harbor they found Faye standing at the dock. Still months later, Faye mentioned to a medical doctor that he had a stiff neck. X-rays showed a broken neck that he received when he bailed out. A severe blow could have severed his spinal cord at any time. But Faye was lucky. After treatment for fifteen months he recovered.

In the days and years to come, armchair strategists in Pearl Harbor, Washington, Newport, and elsewhere would analyze the battle of the Philippine Sea and argue about the results. And they never agreed. Commanders and pilots had no such luxury of time. Their decisions were made in seconds, minutes, or at best hours. Nevertheless, disgruntled airmen claimed that a great opportunity had been lost when Spruance prevented Mitscher from sailing westward on the eighteenth. The fleet had not been sunk. Others vehemently defended Spruance. He had the larger responsibility and acted on the basis of information at hand. No one could say with certainty who was right.

When all was said and done, the battle of the Philippine Sea was a great victory. Although the Japanese fleet had not been sunk, the submarines had been deadly and surviving carriers without aircraft were weapons without power. No one could doubt that Japanese air power had been badly weakened. On June 18, Ozawa had 430 carrier planes. On June 20, he had thirty-five.

Admiral King had no qualms about the battle. The next month he met Spruance at Saipan and told him that he had done exactly the correct thing no matter what the critics might say. He knew that there was never a shortage of critics.

Nimitz said that the squabbles between the airmen and seamen would have to cease. There was still a war to be won and the only thing to do was to get on with the job.

5.

Battle for Leyte Gulf

The largest naval battle in modern history is unleashed in the struggle for the Philippine Islands. Vice Admiral Kinkaid of the Seventh Fleet and Admiral Halsey of the Third Fleet match their wits against Vice Admirals Kurita of the First Striking Force in the center, Nishimura of the Southern Force, and Ozawa of the "Main Body" in the north.

"Bull" Halsey, as the newspapers loved to call him, had made his name in the Solomons where he had become a bright light in the dark, early days of the war. His large head, jutting jaw, bushy eyebrows, and barrel chest, plus an anchor tattooed on his upper right arm, gave him a pugnacious look. Yet he was quick to smile, talked easily, listened to his junior officers, and rallied men around him. Like Lord Nelson, he looked upon the Navy as a "band of brothers." The lowest seaman in the Third Fleet swelled with pride when he said he served under Halsey.

The image was real. Halsey, doggedly determined, was an aggressive and courageous fighter. The son of a naval officer, he was another poor student at Annapolis, but the years that followed turned him into a well-trained, highly professional officer. He was also an aviator. It was true that he had received his wings late in life and did not have Mitscher's extensive experience in aviation, but he was an admiral who fully understood the capability of naval air power.

The appearance of the Third Fleet in the Pacific, like the names of new ships, confused and confounded the Japanese. They wondered if this was a second monstrous armada sailing forth to destroy the Empire. Was it possible? Actually, it was nothing of the sort. Except for a switch in commanders and their staffs, it was a paper change. The ships in both fleets were almost the same. The task forces and groups in the fleet simply changed their numbers. The Fifth Amphibious Force under Turner was now the Third Amphibious Force under Vice Admiral Theodore Wilkinson. Task Force 58 became Task Force 38. But Mitscher was not about to leave, much to the annoyance of his replacement, John McCain, who was impatiently waiting to take over. Mitscher's argument was that he had not been at sea as long as Spruance and his time was not up. It thinly disguised his desire to hold on to a job that he loved, but his argument won. In the back of his head there was undoubtedly the longing to finish off the Japanese fleet. McCain would have to wait.

Under Halsey, the fast carriers continued to grow in numbers even while the battle-damaged *Intrepid* and *Independence* underwent repairs. Now there were sixteen carriers and more would join them later. There were also some changes in the make-up of air groups based upon past experience. The fighters increased because the Hellcats had done so well in living up to their fierce name. They were also versatile and could be used as scouts, and armed with rockets were good ground attack planes. The dive bombers, on the other hand, decreased because troubles with the unstable Helldiver persisted.

Halsey might never function in the same orderly manner

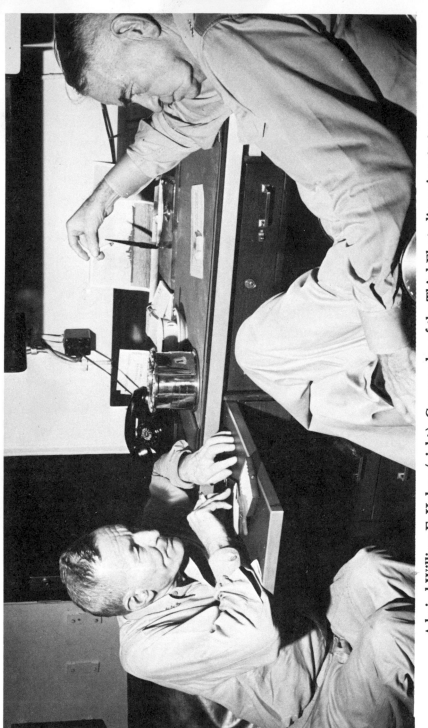

Admiral William F. Halsey (right), Commander of the Third Fleet, discussing strategy of a Pacific operation with Vice Admiral John McCain.

as Spruance, and he might not always hide his emotions, but he had a fine intuitive touch and his decisions were generally sound. Halsey and Spruance were opposites in many ways, but the two old friends only illustrated that it took all kinds to fight a war.

In addition to preinvasion strikes on Peleliu, Halsey struck the airfields in the Philippines to reduce the threat of air attacks from that direction. It was also intended as a softening up process for MacArthur's scheduled landing in Mindanao in the southern end of the islands in November.

Halsey was ready for stiff opposition when his planes hit the Philippines, which were considered one more Japanese stronghold. His sweeps began against the airfields of Mindanao and to his surprise there was less enemy activity than expected. After cleaning up the area, he decided to move the attack to the central Philippines to see if he could find more action. The islands of Leyte, Cebu, Negros, Panay, and Bohol were hit in rapid succession. Again Halsey found little opposition. Carrier planes destroyed more than three hundred aircraft before they got off the ground.

Somewhat amazed, Halsey ordered Mitscher to attack Luzon in the northern Philippines. He knew that there was a major training base for Japanese pilots and an estimated five hundred aircraft there. Still again, the Americans played fast and loose with their weak opponents and wiped them out of the sky. About three hundred more aircraft and twenty-five merchant ships were demolished without the anticipated fray.

Pleased, but puzzled, Halsey studied aerial photographs and reports about enemy strength. One report came from a young ensign who had been shot down over Leyte. Thomas

Tillar from *Hornet's* Air Group 2 had been befriended by Filipinos who told him about the weakness of the Japanese in their islands. When Tillar was picked up by a Navy PBY on rescue duty, he returned to the *Hornet* and his story was relayed to Halsey.

Halsey sat in a corner of the bridge and mulled over the strange situation in his mind. For some time he had suspected that Palau, Yap, and Mindanao were the "vulnerable belly of the Imperial dragon." Now he wondered if the Philippines were ripe for plucking. There was the possibility that thousands of lives could be saved if Palau and Yap were skipped and the date to invade the Philippines advanced. On the other hand, there was nagging uncertainty. He could never be completely sure and, besides, the ships and troops were all set for landing on Peleliu in the Palau group in a couple of days. He asked himself if he could upset the applecart.

Weighing all the facts, Halsey concluded that the Philippines were a "hollow shell." His mind was made up. He told his chief of staff, Mick Carncy, and his flag secretary, Harold Stassen, "I'm going to stick my neck out. Send an urgent dispatch to Cincpac."

On September 13, Halsey radioed Nimitz and recommended that the landing on Peleliu and Yap be canceled and that the forces of the central Pacific combine with MacArthur in the southwest Pacific to invade Leyte.

Nimitz saw the merit in Halsey's idea. He believed, however, that it was too late to stop all the machinery that had been set in motion for Peleliu. As Halsey knew, Wilkinson's Third Amphibious Force with troops packed in dozens of ships was already at sea. Nimitz told Halsey to go ahead with Peleliu while he took another look at Yap and the possibility of moving into Leyte ahead of time.

According to original plans, Leyte was scheduled for invasion on December 20. MacArthur had envisioned landing in Mindanao and then creeping up through the Philippines with a number of intermediate landings with the support of land-based planes much as he had done in New Guinea. Now, when MacArthur learned of Halsey's suggestion, he realized that carrier planes could give him the air cover he needed. He enthusiastically supported Halsey's views.

President Roosevelt and his highest level military advisers were in Quebec attending a meeting with Prime Minister Winston Churchill at the time. Halsey's daring plan came up for discussion before this august group and in almost no time they gave the proposal their approval. The decision was to land in Leyte on October 20, two months ahead of schedule.

Meanwhile, three task groups of TF38 bombed and strafed Peleliu. All of the techniques that had been learned the hard way in previous operations were applied in these strikes. Yet, all of the previous lessons appeared to mean little. The tons of bombs and bullets expended to crush the enemy defense and destroy their will seemed to be wasted. An ingenious network of caves and underground passages, along with enormous concrete pillboxes with heavy guns, shucked off the blasts that came their way. The Japanese will to win was alive and if they lost it would be over their dead bodies.

When the battle-scarred 1st Marine Division landed, another bloody engagement began. Once again, the men on the ground had to slog ahead an inch at a time. The Marine commander said that he would secure the island in four days. He probably thought that if Tarawa fell in four days anything else would be easy. He was wrong. In the first week there were four thousand casualties and it would be months before resistance ceased. It was a shocking revelation that air power had its limits and this last-ditch fighting was a foreboding of things to come. The enemy was down, but not out.

Looking back, it would have been better to have skipped Peleliu as Halsey had suggested. Oddly enough, in the same general operation, a more valuable prize than Peleliu was taken without any opposition. It was Ulithi, 3,660 miles west of Pearl Harbor with a lagoon that was a priceless anchorage large enough to accommodate at least seven hundred ships. Such were the ironies of war.

With the change in plans, Navy commanders and staffs altered course and rushed to Hollandia, New Guinea, to confer with the legendary MacArthur and his men at their headquarters high in the Cyclops Mountains. In less than a month, new schedules had to be set and available forces revised. It was a mammoth pressure job that took long hours and little sleep. There was also a new element. The vast, modern, fast-moving Navy of the central Pacific had to be coordinated with MacArthur's forces that had wearily worked their way through the jungles of New Guinea with slim resources. There was also "MacArthur's Navy," the small Seventh Fleet under Vice Admiral Thomas Kinkaid, that would now expand into an enormous outfit almost overnight.

To the younger officers of the Third Fleet who joined the Seventh Fleet there was a feeling of moving backward in time at Hollandia to another, almost antiquated world. It was a world that had struggled in the backwater with limited supplies and men and had suddenly come into the big time. New faces and new friends had to adjust to the strange ways of each other as they tackled their awesome assignment.

The organization of this combined power was not ideal, but perhaps it was the best that could be arranged on such short notice. General MacArthur was the Supreme Commander Southwest Pacific Area and under him was Kinkaid's Seventh Fleet which would include the Central Philippines Attack Force. A Northern Attack Force under Rear Admiral Daniel Barbey planned to land in the vicinity of the town of Tacloban, and Vice Admiral Wilkinson, shifted from the Third Fleet to the Seventh Fleet for this engagement, would head the Southern Attack Force for a landing in the area of Dulag.

The Attack Forces under Kinkaid also had the support of Rear Admiral Thomas Sprague's escort carriers with three groups known as Taffy 1, Taffy 2, and Taffy 3. As far as it went, the organization was clear and simple for such a grand-scale operation, but it did not include Halsey and the Third Fleet.

Halsey remained under the command of Nimitz. His orders were to cover and support the Leyte invasion by air strikes against Okinawa, Formosa, and Northern Leyte. Then on and after D-Day, he would hit Leyte, Cebu, and Negros, and operate in "strategic support" by destroying enemy naval and air forces that threatened the Philippines.

Halsey's orders also stated, "In case opportunity for destruction of major portion of the enemy fleet is offered or can be created, such destruction becomes the primary task." Such a statement was all Halsey needed. He saw that he was free to pursue the Japanese fleet. Like Spruance and Mitscher, he dearly hoped that he would be the man to sink the enemy Navy once and for all. He had undoubtedly shared Mitscher's view that a great opportunity had been lost at the battle of the Philippine Sea for lack of aggressiveness. No one would ever claim that Halsey was not aggressive.

This split command between Nimitz and MacArthur, and in turn between Halsey and Kinkaid, was against military principle, but it would have to do. Cooperation and coordination must be the key words in the days ahead as they mounted the largest land and sea operation of the Pacific war.

Admiral Toyoda's back was against the wall. Nevertheless, he had seen as clearly as anyone that the next American attack would be in the Philippines. With the loss of the Marianas and Hollandia, it made sense to him that the Americans from the central and southwest Pacific would join forces to invade the Philippines. Where would they land in the Philippines? That was the big question that Toyoda pondered. He would have to wait until the Americans showed their hand.

Toyoda was certain of one thing. He intended to meet the enemy in another do-or-die attempt. The battered and bruised Imperial Fleet would not give up without a fight. Their forces had been badly depleted and yet they had survived in sufficient strength to do serious battle again.

The Imperial General Headquarters developed a series of

Sho-Go plans. "Sho-Go" meant "Victory Operation," and Sho Number 1 was for the defense of the Philippines. These defensive plans left the initiative to the Americans. The strategy depended upon the heavy guns of their battleships and cruisers to destroy the invaders.

The greatest weakness of the Japanese was their lack of trained pilots. It had plagued them since the battle of the Philippine Sea, and the situation had not been corrected. Their one great hope, they thought, was to lure the American fleet away from the beachhead with their carriers. Although the carriers had lost their punch, they still appeared powerful to the Americans. At the time it was not known that the carriers were almost empty of planes.

The Fast Carrier Task Force opened the Leyte campaign, as ordered, with strikes on Okinawa and Luzon, and then attacked Formosa, the headquarters of the Second Air Fleet. These strikes were meant to reduce future interference from land-based planes when the Philippine landings began.

Early on the morning of October 12, radar on Formosa tipped off the Japanese to the approach of American planes and 230 fighters greeted the first carrier strike. Bitter fighting raged over Formosa as the Navy pilots found out this was not another "hollow shell." Vice Admiral Shigeru Fukudome watched planes fall out of the sky and was sure that this was a victorious day for Japan. He was in error. It was a case of mistaken identification. Most of the falling planes were Japanese. However, this was no "Turkey Shoot." The Americans suffered one of their worst days with the loss of forty-eight planes.

The fast carriers were threatened too, as more than a hundred sorties from Formosa were flown against them on the first day. The inexperienced Japanese pilots did little damage, but their exaggerated claims succeeded in deluding their commanders into believing that they had inflicted serious losses.

On Friday, the thirteenth, TF38 struck again and the Japanese retaliated with Betty bombers going after the carriers. One Betty, before being shot down, let go with a torpedo that went straight for the *Franklin*. Captain Shoemaker skillfully rang full speed astern and the torpedo missed its target. A second torpedo headed for the *Franklin* and passed under the stern. Then a bomber, shot down by antiaircraft fire, crashed on the flight deck, slid along the deck, broke into flames, and went overboard into the sea with little damage to the ship. It was all too close for comfort. The crew sighed with relief when the harassed *Franklin* pulled through her bad moments.

The heavy cruiser *Canberra* was not so lucky that day. A torpedo ripped into the side, killed twenty-three men, and opened a hole so large that tons of water surged into the ship before damage control parties halted the flood. The *Wichita* took her in tow and helped her along at a speed of about four knots.

The next day, TF38 sent almost two hundred fifty fighters against Formosa, and again the Japanese fought ferociously. Nevertheless, Admiral Fukudome wrote, "Our fighters were nothing but so many eggs thrown at the stone wall of the indomitable enemy formation." But they did not give up. Hundreds of sorties bore down on the Fast Carrier Task Force and succeeded in torpedoing the light cruiser *Hous-*

The carrier *Franklin* burning after being hit by bombs dropped from Japanese planes.

ton. Two days later, *Houston* took another torpedo and was worse off than *Canberra.* Captain Behrens ordered abandon ship and then, before all the crew was taken off, reversed his order as he fought to keep afloat.

The two cruisers had been so severely damaged that they normally would have been scuttled. Protecting the cripples only hampered the rest of the force. These two ships were not sent under because somebody had a bright idea to create a "Bait Division" to draw out the Japanese fleet. Two light carriers, four cruisers, and thirteen destroyers accompanied the lame ducks and false "distress" messages were sent out. Two carrier groups remained out of sight with the intention of jumping the enemy when they showed up. The rest of the Fast Carrier Task Force withdrew at high speed.

The reports of their own pilots had given the Japanese the impression that they had inflicted serious damage. Now they learned of the retreating remnants of TF38. This seemed like the opportunity they had long awaited.

Rear Admiral Laurance DuBose, commander of what was called "CripDiv 1," anxiously waited for the worst. Playing the part of the bait was not exactly fun.

Halsey sent a message to DuBose, "Don't worry!" DuBose replied to Halsey, "Not worrying, just wondering and waiting." Captain Inglis of the *Birmingham,* one of the supporting cruisers, said to DuBose, "Now I know how a worm on a fishhook must feel."

It was a good idea. Vice Admiral Shima's Second Striking Force with heavy cruisers *Nachi* and *Ashigara* set out for the bait. Unfortunately, a Japanese reconnaissance plane spotted the two carrier groups lying in wait and the attackers quickly reversed their course. It was a nice try that almost worked.

By now the *Houston*'s condition had grown worse. More than six thousand tons of the Pacific Ocean poured into the ship. No vessel had ever remained afloat in such shape. Most of the crew was taken off. Still, damage control parties continued to work and eventually she would reach a safe haven along with *Canberra* at Ulithi.

The Formosa air battle was a rough prelude to the Philippine invasion. As D-Day approached ever closer, the fast carrier planes pounded Luzon while Kinkaid's escort carriers bombed Leyte airfields, and six old battleships bombarded the shore. The strikes paid off. On October 20, the men on the hundreds of amphibious craft were pleased to find little air activity when they sailed into Leyte Gulf.

It was an especially big day for Douglas MacArthur. The dream that he had sought for almost three discouraging years had come true. He kept his promise as he waded ashore from his landing boat amid clicking cameras and said to his chief of staff, "Well, believe it or not, we're here." Deeply touched, the general made a brief speech on the beach and said, "People of the Philippines, I have returned. By the grace of Almighty God our forces stand again on Philippine soil. . . . Let the indomitable spirit of Bataan and Corregidor lead on."

The landing of the Sixth Army proceeded smoothly with relatively little action on the beaches. Leyte, however, was a huge island that produced vast quantities of sugar cane, rice, hemp, and corn. Oil, manganese, and sulphur were among its rich resources and the population was climbing toward the million mark. Inland there would be many sharp battles before the American Army completely controlled the island. Leyte, like the atolls, was another stepping stone. It would become a base for tackling Luzon, the most important island of the Philippines.

While troops efficiently streamed onto the beaches, naval commanders asked themselves if the Japanese fleet would really come out of hiding. Most of them had probably thought that they would not see the fleet at Leyte. Some had thought there might be a few "hit and run" raids. They were only opinions without facts. By D-Day, they started to change their minds.

Now that the United States Army and Navy had committed their forces, Toyoda acted decisively. Three main units, a center, southern, and northern force, would operate under his command. The First Striking Force would operate in the center of the Philippines. It was the most powerful collection of battleships and cruisers that the Japanese had assembled during the entire war. The superships *Musashi* and *Yamato*, the largest warships in the world, were accompanied by five other battleships, thirteen cruisers, and nineteen destroyers. The able Vice Admiral Takeo Kurita commanded these ships that departed from Lingga Roads off Singapore. Well-aware of the risks, he planned to wind his way through the treacherous waters of the central Philippines, exit from San Bernardino Strait, and enter Leyte Gulf off the island of Samar.

A southern force, under Vice Admiral Shoji Nishimura, was made up of two battleships, *Fuso* and *Yamashiro*, a heavy cruiser, and four destroyers. Vice Admiral Shima's three cruisers and four destroyers that had turned away from chasing the Bait Division would also lend support. They would approach Leyte Gulf by sailing through Surigao Strait in the south. If all went well, the center and southern forces would execute a perfect pincer movement that would obliterate the American amphibious forces.

A northern force, commanded by the experienced Vice Admiral Ozawa, consisted of the feeble carriers. Four carriers, the hybrid battleship/carriers *Ise* and *Hyuga*, three light cruisers, and eight destroyers would leave Japan. It was called the "Main Body," but this was misleading. With the carrier power exhausted, its purpose was to serve as the decoy to attract the United States Third Fleet away from the action at Leyte Gulf. The tactics of entrapment had always appealed to the Japanese. Yet Ozawa knew that this trap, if successful, would end in suicide for the Japanese.

The geography of the Philippines created a perfect setting for a classical naval battle and Toyoda planned to use it to the fullest advantage. This was no hit and run. The greatest naval engagement in modern history was in the making.

Bits of information started to trickle in from sighting reports that gave Halsey and Kinkaid strong hints of a brewing battle. Once again, the fearless submarines were superb. Two boats, *Dace* and *Darter*, spotted Kurita's center force in Palawan Passage and with magnificent marksmanship sunk two heavy cruisers and damaged a third. It was now clear that the Japanese were coming out for a fight.

By October 20, neither Halsey nor Kinkaid had any doubts that the two enemy forces from the center and south were moving in on Leyte Gulf. At the moment, however, they had not heard about the northern force of carriers.

Early on the twenty-fourth, a search plane sighted Kurita's flagship, the mammoth *Yamato*, bound for San Bernardino

Strait. Halsey, operating offshore to the north of Kinkaid, retained tactical command in his own hands and sent orders to go after the center force directly to the fast carrier task group commanders. This bypassed Mitscher and placed him in an awkward position of having little to do at a crucial time. The aggressive Halsey would have been wiser if he had used Mitscher as his tactical commander. He had far greater experience in handling this complicated, modern outfit. Things had changed since the old days when Halsey was in the Solomons.

While air strikes went out against the center force in the Sibuyan Sea, the fast carriers fought off attacks from land-based planes. Commander David McCampbell, the leading Navy air ace, who had been a standout at the "Turkey Shoot," put in another busy day protecting the task force. His group from the *Essex* shot down or chased off more than fifty planes.

McCampbell had an altitude edge during ninety-five minutes of combat that he used to good advantage. He followed the weaving fighters and knocked down those that attempted to climb to his altitude. His group made eighteen to twenty passes and were careful not to expose themselves or waste ammunition until they were at very close range. It was almost a case of not firing until they saw "the whites of their eyes." McCampbell shot down at least nine planes himself.

Princeton's air group handled their interceptions well too. Unfortunately, a Judy bomber came out of the clouds without detection and dropped a bomb on the light carrier. Fierce fires led to torpedo explosions and the *Princeton*'s after elevator blew up. Damage control parties remained aboard, but all others abandoned ship. Many of the crew jumped overboard and drowned in a rough sea. Some of the stronger swimmers reached cargo nets that destroyers had cast over the side and they climbed to safety.

The cruiser *Birmingham* arrived to join the firefighters and thirty-eight volunteers led by Lieutenant Allan Reed boarded the flaming carrier. The destroyer *Morrison*, on the lee side, picked up four hundred survivors. Then heavy debris started falling on her decks from the *Princeton* and the crew had the strange and frightening sensation of seeing a jeep and electric airplane tractor fly through the air and land in their midst.

At the time the bomb hit, two captains were on board the *Princeton*. Soon, Bill Buracker was scheduled to be relieved by John M. Hoskins. The change, however, had not yet taken place.

In the bombing, Hoskins's foot was severely smashed. When the ship's doctor, who was also wounded, examined the foot he decided that the only thing to do was to cut it off. He performed the operation with only a sheath knife.

Hoskins, a man with plenty of intestinal fortitude, did not let the handicap stand in his way. By the time a new *Princeton* was ready for combat, Hoskins had a new artificial foot and he recommended himself for the command. He wrote that he was "one foot ahead of the other applicants." He received the command and still later became a rear admiral.

During the rush of the rescue work, a second air raid, a rough sea, and a submarine alert added extra strain to an already strenuous situation. Hindrances to the contrary, progress continued until a colossal explosion in a torpedo stowage blew off most of the *Princeton*'s stern and after flight deck.

In the blast the *Birmingham* lost more lives than the *Princeton*. Steel parts crashed onto the deck and slashed into the rescuers. Dead and dying crowded the decks. In seconds, 229 men had been killed and more than 400 wounded. Streams of blood flowed down the waterways. Stunned men found that they had lost an arm or leg and amid the horror quietly waited for help. The more fortunate moved among the wounded and aided the one doctor and medical corpsmen. When the worst was over, the captain gave orders for burial at sea.

The most somber ceremony in the Navy was repeated many times in the Pacific. With the ship's company on deck, the captain or chaplain would read the solemn service and when the ritual reached the words, "We commit this body to the deep," a seaman would tilt the platform and the body would slip from under the American flag into the ocean.

The *Birmingham* had fought hard to save the *Princeton* and in a sense succeeded. The ship remained afloat, but no ship could be spared to take her in tow. Reluctantly, Captain Buracker ordered everyone off the ship and the cruiser *Reno* finished the *Princeton* with torpedoes.

All this went on while Halsey's mind was centered on Kurita's force that threatened to destroy the Leyte landing. During the morning and early afternoon of the twenty-fourth, Halsey had sent planes from three task groups to sink Kurita's ships. The fourth task group had been sent out of the area to refuel. For the past two months the fast carrier squadrons had been making one strike after another. The pilots, near exhaustion, had difficulty eating and sleeping as the tension grew. They were also slower, less accurate, and more accident prone. Mitscher said that in the past ten months there were probably ten thousand men in the task force who had not been ashore except for some atoll like Ulithi. Nevertheless, the strikes continued and by the end of the day, 259 sorties were flown. No effort was spared.

The Japanese had almost no air cover. Nonetheless, they sent up unmerciful antiaircraft fire against the first strike that the *Intrepid* and *Cabot* had launched. Nineteen fighters, twelve bombers, and thirteen torpedo planes led by Commander William Ellis dove into the heavy flak. Bursts of pink with streamers, purple bursts, white tracers, an abundance of white phosphorus, and a new shell which burst and ejected silver pellets, clouded the sky. Two Avengers were hit and landed in the water. One fighter crashed in flames.

For hours bombs and torpedoes dropped on the advancing force. The giant *Musashi*, with her 18.1-inch guns, was the bull's-eye for the carrier pilots. Was it possible for aircraft to sink such a monster? Hit again and again, she finally rolled over and sank. Other ships were damaged, but the exact extent of the damage was not known. It was positive knowledge, however, that Kurita had reversed course and appeared to be in retreat.

Halsey was overjoyed with the good news and readily accepted the claims of the pilots. Mitscher, more experienced and more skeptical about pilot reports, had his doubts about the total damage. Halsey, however, did not ask for Mitscher's advice.

Although Halsey was optimistic, he realized that Kurita might pull his forces together, turn around, and advance again, so he sent a battle plan to his commanders to meet that possible event. He radioed that four of the six fast battleships, two heavy and three light carriers, and fourteen destroyers "will be formed as TF34 under V. Adm. Lee, Commander Battle Line." Halsey did not send this message to Kinkaid, but Kinkaid was aware of the plan because his communications people had intercepted the message. Kinkaid was pleased to learn that Halsey was ready to cut off the center threat if it bounced back. He assumed, as most officers did who read the dispatch, including Nimitz at Pearl Harbor, that TF34 had been formed.

Since the center and southern forces did not have carrier support, the whereabouts of the enemy carriers became the disturbing element in the minds of the admirals. Where were they? Would they attack from some other quarter? Ozawa, coming from the north with his carriers, did his best to be sighted. He sent out false radio transmissions and search planes in the hope that they would give his position away and attract Halsey. So far, he was not doing very well as a decoy. Nothing seemed to work. War was perverse.

Late in the afternoon, TF38 planes finally located Ozawa's ships. They were only 190 miles away. This was what Halsey had been looking for, a chance to destroy the air power of the Japanese Navy. He would not, he thought, make the same mistake as Spruance. He would take the initiative. "Get the carriers" had been engraved on every airman's mind.

That evening, Halsey and his staff talked over the possibility of leaving Lee and his battleships to guard San Bernardino Strait while he took off after the carriers. TF34 had not been formed as Kinkaid believed. Halsey's misleading, poorly phrased dispatch had only announced a preparatory plan. Now, when the time of execution arrived, he decided to keep his fleet together. He wanted maximum strength. And he was sure in his mind that the center force of Kurita's had been rendered incapable of doing any more harm. TF34 would not be formed. "We will run north at top speed," he said, "and put those carriers out for keeps."

It all seemed perfectly reasonable and Halsey followed sound naval doctrine when he decided not to split his forces. At 2006, Halsey learned that Kurita was not so harmless. He had turned around again and was headed for San Bernardino Strait. The news of Kurita's revival did not shake Halsey's determination. He believed Kinkaid could handle Kurita's weakened force. His plans remained the same and he went to bed after almost two nights without sleep. Admirals, like pilots, rarely received enough rest. Their most important decisions were made when they were the most exhausted.

Kinkaid learned that the center force was on the move again too. He also knew that Halsey intended to go after the northern force of carriers. But he felt no qualms. He was sure that the battle line of TF34 could deal with any threat around San Bernardino Strait. Communications between Halsey and Kinkaid were a bare minimum and each man made assumptions that were not always correct about what the other man would do. Then too, Halsey was a man of action, not words. At best, his orders were customarily vague.

At midnight, when the task groups of TF38 gathered for the northern attack, Mitscher was surprised to learn that the TF34 battle line had not been formed. Halsey was running the show and he was almost out of the picture. Arleigh Burke and Jimmy Flatley, the operations officer, woke Mitscher and urged him to recommend that Halsey send the battleships back to guard San Bernardino Strait. They had received a report that the center force was "still very much afloat and still moving toward San Bernardino." Mitscher asked, "Does

Task Force 38 entering anchorage in line; the *Langley*,
Ticonderoga, and *Washington* leading the way.

Halsey have that report?" Flatley said, "Yes." Mitscher replied, "If he wants my advice, he'll ask for it."

In the meantime, the situation in Leyte Gulf grew taut.
Kinkaid had sent Admiral Oldendorf and his old battleships
to meet the southern force at Surigao Strait. Five of the six
battleships that steamed south had been resurrected from
Pearl Harbor. It would be a long night.

During the dark hours, thirty-nine little PT boats waited in
and near the strait. Their orders were to make contact reports
when they sighted the enemy, attack, and then clear out of
the way for the destroyer runs. The PT boats had gained a
tremendous reputation in the early days of the war in the
Philippines. Newspapers had made great claims for them
and a popular book had said that they were "expendable."
Actually, they had seen little action since the Solomons and
their miscellaneous duties had become boring. Tonight they
would not be bored.

The PTs were invaluable because night radar-equipped
planes were not available. At 2250, some of the boats sighted
the enemy. While they attempted to make their contact reports, the destroyer *Shigure's* searchlight spotted them and
started firing. The speedboats zigzagged, but PT-152 was hit.
One man was killed and three wounded. Another shell went
through PT-130 and knocked out the radio, but she rushed
to the next section and relayed her message. This was the first
definite information about the enemy that Oldendorf received that night.

As the huge Japanese ships advanced through the strait,
thirty of the brave little PTs took them on in the glare of
searchlights. Exposed and under heavy gunfire, the fragile
boats made their speedy torpedo runs. Before the night was

over one PT would hit the cruiser *Abukuma*. The others had little success, but they distracted the approaching enemy and their accurate sighting reports were priceless.

Next came the destroyers. Fast and far more powerful, Captain Jesse Coward's Destroyer Squadron 54 made a torpedo attack in the classic War College manner while enemy starshells, green flares, and searchlights sought them out. The *Remey*, in an unwanted spotlight, made the crew feel "like animals in a cage." In the frantic minutes that followed five enemy ships were hit.

Captain K. M. McMannes's Destroyer Squadron 24 had the next crack at the enemy. He sailed into the hail of gunfire and in two minutes the battleship *Yamashiro* was hit. The Japanese, in disarray, pressed onward.

Destroyer Squadron 56, under Captain Roland Smoot, made a "column right" and moved in close at maximum speed. As his ships made their runs, the rear destroyer *Albert W. Grant* was hit. A wounded torpedoman's mate launched her remaining torpedoes while the ship took eighteen more hits, some from a "friendly" light cruiser. Thirty-four men were killed and ninety-four wounded. To make matters worse, the doctor and one of the pharmacist's mates were among the first killed. Commander Terrell Nisewaner, the captain, and others, knowing the danger of men being burned alive, groped their way through the fiery engine room and pulled out everyone they could find. Machinist's mate, second class, D. W. Barnes used his bare hands to smother some of the flames on scorched men.

Heroism, known only to the men on board, finally brought the ship under control. And in these narrow waters that left

106

little room for maneuvering, the destroyer *Newcomb* came alongside and hauled her clear.

Behind the destroyers were the cruisers and battleships. Oldendorf had formed his battle line and that night he accomplished what every Admiral dreamed about as a wild ambition. He "crossed the T." As the remaining enemy column sailed into his line, the *West Virginia, Tennessee,* and *California* fired salvo after salvo of fourteen- and sixteen-inch shells with deadly accuracy. *Maryland* got off six salvos and *Mississippi* managed one. They were doing their savage best to avenge Pearl Harbor.

By dawn, both Japanese battleships had been sunk, and by 1000 Nishimura's force had been wiped out except for the lucky *Shigure*. Shima, coming up from the rear, saw the destruction and retreated. It was almost a clean sweep for Oldendorf, who had fought what was undoubtedly the last naval engagement in history without air power.

In the quiet that followed the battle, destroyers, under orders, sailed toward the small boats and bobbing heads in the water to pick up Japanese survivors. The devout sailors showed little interest in these humane efforts. Captain Thomas Conley in the *Robinson* said, "The survivors in the water seemed bent on ignoring us completely and few of them would glance directly at the ship." When the *Halford* approached a small boat to help, the Japanese jumped overboard. They preferred to perish.

The morning of the twenty-fifth, the situation seemed well in hand as Kinkaid's escort carriers off Leyte Gulf carried on with their duties. These were Taffy 1, 2, and 3 spread out over a 120-mile area under the command of Rear Admiral

Thomas Sprague who also directed Taffy 1. Rear Admiral Felix Stump commanded Taffy 2, and Rear Admiral Clifton Sprague, no relation, who was known as "Ziggy," commanded Taffy 3, the northernmost group off Samar.

Early morning searches were the first order of the day. Nothing unusual was expected, but at 0646, radarmen on the *Fanshaw Bay* in Taffy 3 picked up an unidentified surface contact and radiomen heard Japanese on the interfighter direction net. A minute later, Ensign Hans Jensen, on antisubmarine patrol, saw four Japanese battleships, eight cruisers, and a number of destroyers. They were only twenty miles from Taffy 3. Jensen made a bombing attack on a cruiser. It was unbelievable. Did Jensen make a mistake? The call went out to check identification. All doubts vanished as the pagodalike masts of the battleships and cruisers appeared on the horizon.

These were the ships that Halsey had supposedly covered at San Bernardino. Kurita was as surprised as the CVE commanders. What had he run into? Was he up against TF38? He did not know that these were small escort carriers. Confusion reigned among the Japanese as Kurita gave the order to attack.

The thin-skinned, slow-moving CVEs were no match for this powerful force. "Ziggy" Sprague opened his range, launched every plane fit to fly, made smoke, and called for help. Sprague wanted to slow down the enemy while making his halfway escape.

At 0707, Kinkaid radioed Halsey in plain language that his ships were under heavy attack. Halsey did not receive the message for more than an hour.

In the meantime, Halsey was on his way north that morning as the battle off Samar unfolded. Kinkaid anxiously sought help. It was hard for him to believe that TF34 had not covered San Bernardino Strait. Kinkaid radioed Halsey again, "Urgently need BBs (battleships) Leyte Gulf at once."

The message astounded Halsey. He had his own battle to fight. Besides, he thought, Kinkaid had his old battleships for protection. But the old battleships to the south were three hours away from the scrap off Samar.

Other messages from Kinkaid brought little response, partly because of delays in transmission. Finally, Kinkaid sent another message in plain language looking for the commander of the fast battleships. It was too urgent to worry about codes:

WHERE IS LEE X SEND LEE.

At Pearl Harbor, Nimitz followed events every step of the way and wondered where Lee was too. He could not restrain himself any longer and sent Halsey a similar message. As usual, the communicators padded their messages with meaningless prefixes and suffixes to confound the enemy. This was standard practice. Nimitz's message read:

TURKEY TROTS TO WATER GG FROM CINCPAC . . . X WHERE
IS RPT WHERE IS TASK FORCE THIRTY-FOUR RR THE WORLD
WONDERS.

The last three words, "the world wonders," were a part of the padding, but the typist in the communications room of Halsey's flagship, *New Jersey*, left it as part of the dispatch that Halsey read.

Incensed by the apparent insult from Nimitz, Halsey felt like he had been struck in the face. He threw his cap on the deck and was so emotional that his chief of staff, Mick Carney, had to calm him down. "Stop it," he said. "What the hell's the matter with you? Pull yourself together." Halsey was only about forty minutes away from Ozawa's carriers and he intended to finish them off with his battleships. The embers glowed inside him, but he reluctantly sent his six fast battleships and one of the carrier groups south to help Kinkaid. They would arrive too late to be useful. Halsey continued his pursuit of Ozawa.

The little escort carriers and their screen remained on their own. Stump, with Taffy 2, was nearest Sprague and he shouted into the TBS, "Don't be alarmed, Ziggy—remember, we're back of you—don't get excited, don't do anything rash." Stump sent off his planes to help. So did the other Sprague.

"Ziggy" Sprague kept cool in these hot waters. Salvos splashed everywhere. It seemed impossible for the ships to survive. He ordered the screen of destroyers to make torpedo attacks, and then, for about ten minutes he hid under the protection of a heaven-sent rain squall.

Taffy 3 destroyers, *Hoel*, *Heermann*, and *Johnston*, made a mad dash for the enemy. *Johnston* led the way, fired ten torpedoes, and retired. At least one torpedo hit the cruiser *Kumano*. A battleship and cruiser opened up on *Johnston* and knocked out the after fire room and engine room. Their gyro compass was ruined, and radar equipment on the mast crashed onto the bridge. The deck was riddled with shell holes. Commander Ernest Evans, the captain, had his shirt

110

and two fingers on his right hand blown off. It did not stop him.

Hoel attacked the *Kumano* and sent a half-salvo of torpedoes at the battleship *Kongo* and suffered severe damage too. *Heermann,* in the same daring company, took on the battleship *Kongo* and almost everything else in sight at flank speed. Cutting through the heavy smoke she missed the *Johnston* "by about three inches." Deck crews on both ships sent up a spontaneous cheer.

Hoel took over forty hits from battleships, cruisers, and destroyers. The major caliber shells from the heavy ships went right through her, but she was becoming more like a sieve below the water line. Somehow she managed to fire another half-salvo and probably hit a heavy cruiser. At 0835, the crew abandoned ship. Twenty minutes later she sank.

The *Roberts,* a small destroyer escort, tackled the heavy cruiser column, fired three torpedoes, and retired without a scratch. Other destroyer escorts did their best to divert the attention of the cruisers in this delaying action. *Roberts's* luck did not last. After a gallant battle, she sank with the loss of eighty-nine men.

The *Johnston* shared the fate of the *Roberts.* Evans had been in the thick of it, firing on one ship after another to cause confusion and to keep the enemy from closing on the carriers. His ship was so badly damaged he finally commanded the ship from the stern and gave steering orders through an open hatch to men who were turning the rudder by hand. Surrounded by a circling Japanese destroyer squadron "like Indians attacking a prairie schooner," they were overwhelmed. One of the *Johnston* survivors swimming in the water noticed the captain of one of the enemy destroyers salute as the bold *Johnston* went down. More than half of the crew was killed. Evans was alive in the water, but disappeared before help arrived.

At great sacrifice to themselves, the destroyers and destroyer escorts had succeeded in stalling for time and forced the enemy into evasive action. Kurita's chief of staff later wrote, "The enemy destroyers coordinated perfectly to cover the inferior speed of the escort carriers. They bravely launched torpedoes to intercept us, and they embarrassed us by putting up a dense smoke screen."

The CVEs did not get off scot free. The *Kalinin Bay* was hit by a heavy cruiser and she responded by firing her one five-inch gun. Later, *Kalinin Bay* would take more severe blows. Despite poor shooting, the *Fanshaw Bay*, *White Plains*, and *Gambier Bay* were also hit. *Gambier Bay* took the worst beating. Hit repeatedly by full salvos, she was finally abandoned. Lieutenant William Buderous of the *Gambier Bay* helped many of the men in the water to rafts and then refused to take a place in an overcrowded one. He held onto the side until he was torn to pieces by a shark.

Meanwhile, the escort carrier aircraft had plunged into the enemy ships. They were ill-equipped for such a task because they were armed for combat air patrol, antisubmarine search, and support of infantry. Most of them did not normally carry heavy bombs and torpedoes. Some of the planes armed with torpedoes made successful runs while others, unarmed, merely made dummy runs to distract the enemy.

Despite shortcomings, fighters and torpedo bombers attacked with all of their available might. They strafed, bombed, and rocketed. Lieutenant (j.g.) L. E. Waldrop, pilot of a torpedo plane, accomplished a million-to-one shot. He strafed a torpedo headed for the carriers and it exploded. And yet, it all seemed like a hopeless cause. It was a matter of time, and soon the persistent and powerful Japanese were bound to overtake them.

At 0925, while "Ziggy" Sprague was busy dodging torpedoes, a disappointed signalman yelled, "They're getting away." The astonished admiral, far less disappointed, could not believe his eyes, but the Japanese fleet was retiring. He said, "It took a whole series of reports from circling planes to convince me. And still I could not get the fact to soak into my battle-numbed brain. At best, I had expected to be swimming by this time."

Kurita was under the impression that he had run into part of TF38. He also had another report that there were more carriers to the north of him. News arrived from the *Shigure* too, that it was the only ship left in Nishimura's force. And by now, he believed that the American transports had escaped from Leyte Gulf. He feared a trap and saw no point in pressing on. He decided to turn back and attack the enemy carriers to the north, but his report was false and he never found them.

Kurita had sailed away from a sure victory and the CVEs were miraculously saved. Their combined air and sea efforts had not only won a delaying action, but also had sunk three heavy cruisers.

But the CVEs were not out of trouble. About two hours later, when they were breathing a little easier, nine planes approached them from a low altitude that escaped radar detection. Then they climbed higher, evaded interceptors, and, without wavering, made direct descents upon four carriers. These pilots had no intention of dropping bombs. They crashed into the ships with their bombs. The first three ships narrowly escaped severe damage. The fourth, *St. Lo*, which had not been touched that morning, took a solid smash on the flight deck. Fires set off explosions and the *St. Lo* sank.

Four *St. Lo* pilots, unable to land on their carrier, set their flak-ridden planes down on the airstrip at Dulag on Leyte just as the Japanese counterattacked. Soldiers gave three of the pilots a carbine and foxhole and told them to fire on the enemy. They were a little out of their element, but they did as they were told. Eventually, the pilots, using buckets, refueled their planes, rearmed, and returned to other carriers.

Isolated suicide dives had occurred throughout the war. This attack was different. It was a reserve force established by Vice Admiral Takijiro Onishi in Luzon. Desperately short of experienced pilots, Onishi organized the Kamikaze Special Attack Corps to give pilots the honor of sacrificing themselves for their country. Suicide pilots also attacked the CVEs *Santee* and *Suwanee* in Taffy 1. The Special Attack Corps had just begun its work. "Kamikaze" would become a familiar word in the Pacific.

To the north Halsey now had the opportunity to sink the enemy carriers that had been the Navy goal throughout the war. He had no way of knowing at the time that the enemy carriers were only the weak remains of their former power. The battle took place off Cape Engaño. "Engaño" is a Spanish word for "mistake, deception, or lure."

Halsey gave the tactical command to Mitscher on the twenty-fifth and the planes were off early. Search planes had difficulty finding the exact location of the enemy force until two junior intelligence officers on Mitscher's staff insisted that the Japanese carriers were to the east of the scheduled search sectors. The officers were Lieutenants E. Calvert Cheston and Byron "Whizzer" White. White had been at Guadalcanal earlier and was admired throughout the Pacific because he was both a Rhodes Scholar and professional football player. Many years later he would become a member of the Supreme Court of the United States.

McCampbell of Air Group 15 directed the first strike against the four carriers. Ozawa could only fight back with a few planes and the weak air defense seemed strange to Halsey. The *Chitose*, attacked by bombers, was the first to go down, and then *Chiyoda* was abandoned.

Weak air strength or not, Ensign George Denby of Air Group 20 was hit by a Zeke and bailed out. On the way down, he dangled by his right leg until he was able to straighten himself out. In the water he found that the front half of his life jacket was ripped. The back half remained inflated as long as he kept orally blowing it up every half-hour. Soon he found that he had company. Sharks, four to five feet long, swam close by but never bothered him unless he stopped kicking. One grazed his leg without doing any harm.

Denby's tongue and lips swelled and after two hours it looked like the end was near. Then a destroyer approached so close, the propeller wash forced him under twice. The destroyer threw Denby two lines and by that time he was too weak to hold on. A crew member dived into the water, fastened the lines under Denby's arms, and brought him on board.

Carrier Strike Force

In the afternoon, Commander Hugh Winters of Air Group 19 from the *Lexington* and Commander Malcolm Wordell of Air Group 44 from the *Langley* put an end to the infamous *Zuikaku* and *Zuiho*. Still later, cruisers under DuBose pursued and sank the wounded *Chitose*.

Kurita and Nishimura had failed. Ozawa succeeded as a decoy, but the carriers in his force vanished. In the final tally for the entire battle on three fronts, the Japanese had lost three battleships, four carriers, nine cruisers and eight destroyers. The United States had lost the light carrier *Princeton*, two escort carriers, two destroyers, one destroyer escort, and one PT boat.

Was Halsey right in turning north to seek the carriers? He never admitted he was wrong and he had many defenders. However, he gave a clue to his feelings when he said, "I wish that Spruance had been with Mitscher at Leyte Gulf and I had been with Mitscher in the battle of the Philippine Sea."

The armchair strategists, ever-wise with their hindsight, have debated the pros and cons ever since and it will never be settled to everyone's satisfaction. Both Kinkaid and Halsey, being human, made mistakes, but they made tough decisions under great pressure, as Spruance had done before them. The only sure thing is that another great victory had been won. It was a great victory, not a perfect victory. There are no such things.

6.

Typhoon

The Third Fleet meets an enemy more relentless than the Japanese Imperial Fleet.

TF38 had little rest after the Battle of Leyte Gulf. When the flight surgeon on the *Wasp* examined the pilots of Air Group 14, he found only thirty of 131 pilots fit for combat. Similar situations existed in other air groups. Fatigue had taken its toll. Yet there was little rest for the weary.

By November, Halsey said, "I was tired in mind, in body, and nerves." The Army Air Force was unable to give the struggling infantrymen on Leyte the close support that they needed and the fast carriers had been ordered to remain offshore to lend a hand. MacArthur saw the value of their precision bombing. Still, it was a costly operation.

The Navy found itself in a strange position. They had just won the greatest sea battle in history, and now, more than ever before, started thinking about defensive tactics. The reason was the intensified activity of the kamikazes. Halsey thought that the tension created by the threat of attacks was worse than the actual attacks. While on station, his day began about 0500 when he watched the first strikes take off, and ended about midnight after a final check of the charts and dispatches in flag plot. Then he retired to his sea cabin, had his tenth cup of coffee and fortieth cigarette, and hoped he might have five hours sleep. He rarely did.

The suicide pilots may have been an act of desperation,

but they were a more effective weapon than anyone wanted to admit. Training of pilots had been the great Japanese weakness in air strength. Now, they had no need to train raw pilots. All they had to do was head them in the right direction.

The list of damaged carriers grew. The *Franklin, Belleau Wood, Lexington, Intrepid, Essex,* and *Cabot* were among those hit as the casualties mounted.

In October, Vice Admiral John McCain took command of TF38 and the weary Mitscher went home on leave. He would be missed. After a rest, however, he would rejoin Spruance and plan future operations for the Fifth Fleet.

McCain looked and acted like the old sea dog that he was. Like Mitscher, McCain was small, high-strung, and had a well-weathered face. Unlike Mitscher, he blew up from time to time to let off pressure. His language was certainly salty and he rolled his cigarettes, making a mess with the tobacco, fidgeted, and acted like a jumping jack.

Naval officers, especially junior officers, took great pride in the greenish patina that collected on the gold braid and eagle device on their hats after months at sea. It announced that they were veterans. McCain outdid them all with a hat that the amused Halsey called an affront to Navy regulations. It was a green drab fatigue cap on the visor of which his wife had sewn "scrambled eggs." The crown was threadbare and the visor showed the worst effects of sea air. McCain considered it his lucky combat hat, and of course he knew it entertained the men.

McCain had been waiting in the wings a long time for a chance to lead the Fast Carrier Task Force. In actuality, however, Halsey ran the fast carriers and McCain was merely his lieutenant. It was not the same careful team of Spruance and Mitscher.

In December, Halsey and McCain faced another enemy more relentless than the Japanese Imperial Fleet. Its power exceeded man-made forces and struck terror in the hearts of all seamen.

After three days of air strikes against Luzon, TF38 was low on fuel and set out east of the Philippines beyond the range of the Japanese for a rendezvous with their oilers. Fueling began on December 17. The weather was foul for the delicate job of transferring fuel from one ship to another, but far from dangerous. Three days before, the pilot of a search plane had reported a tropical disturbance southeast of Samar and yet this seemed a long way off and of little consequence.

Unknown to Halsey, or the aerologist (the person responsible for the atmospheric meteorology) on the *New Jersey*, or the aerologists on board each carrier, a firm typhoon was on the way. The northerly wind and sea of thirty to forty knots gave no sign of worse to come. As it was, fueling was slow and troublesome. Parted hoses, near-collisions, and the need to lash down planes made plenty of extra work. By 1500 on the seventeenth, escort carriers could not recover two planes and the pilots received orders to bail out. It took enormous courage for the pilots to parachute down into the dark sea. Drowning must have seemed almost a certainty. Fortunately, a destroyer fished them out of the water with great efficiency.

Signs of dangerous weather had definitely showed up. Halsey ordered his ships to stop fueling and steam to another rendezvous so that they could continue to fuel the next day. Based on the available data, it appeared that the storm would clear them on this course. What they did not know was that the center of this small but powerful typhoon was much closer than assumed. It was only 120 miles southeast, not 450 miles, as the *New Jersey* aerologist had estimated. Other aerologists in the task force made estimates that were equally inaccurate. Nevertheless, Captain J. T. Acuff, commander of the fueling group, made a pretty good guess and Halsey changed the rendezvous area again. Conditions improved on the new course, or so it seemed, for a while.

The fleet stretched out for miles and not all the ships experienced the same weather. By evening, however, the sea was pitch black. Carriers headed into the wind, rose above the high waves, and then crashed into the sea with an impact that threatened to shake the planes loose. Lookouts were ordered below, and everything on deck was doubly lashed.

By midnight, the barometer was at a low 29.76 on the *New Jersey* and the wind blew twenty-eight knots. It was rough, but not alarming. A fourth rendezvous was now set. Halsey ordered all carriers and escorts to change course to due south, and later to northwest, in the hope of finding easier sailing. This was a mistake. It took many of the ships straight into the way of the approaching typhoon.

The bad weather increased and the realization of serious storm conditions was now evident, and yet estimates continued to be erroneous. Now the fourth rendezvous area was canceled. The ships sailed south and would fuel when possible. Halsey, with an upcoming landing at Mindoro on his mind, had done his best to refuel. By 0803 on December 18, he gave up such hopes.

The wind rose to forty-three knots, the barometer fell to 29.61, and disturbing messages started to reach the *New Jersey*. At 0907, the *Independence* reported a man overboard. A few minutes later, the light carrier *Monterey* reported that planes on the hangar deck had broken loose and caught fire during a bad roll. At 0942, the escort carrier *Kwajalein* had lost steering control.

Around 1000, the barometer plummeted and the wind moved counter-clockwise, sure signs of a typhoon. At 1007, the wind was sixty-two knots, the barometer 29.52. About noon, McCain ordered TF38 to steer a course 120 degrees, a wise decision because it took the fleet away from the storm center. But it was too late for some of the ships to get out of harm's way.

Between 1100 and 1400, the typhoon did its worst and the great ships, the highest technology of modern man, were like toys as they tossed about in seventy-foot waves. The wind velocity increased to eighty-three knots with gusts over one hundred knots. The barometer was down to 29.23. The *Wasp* reported a low of 29.1, and the needles on barometers of other ships momentarily swung lower. At 1210, the *Dewey* rolled 65 degrees to starboard, 75 degrees to port. The barometer needle went off the scale at 27.

The winds howled and whined and blinding rain made it impossible to tell the ocean from the air. Halsey said that the *New Jersey* was once hit by a five-inch shell and he was not aware that it had happened. A suicide plane crashed into the main deck of the fast battleship *Missouri* and the damage was repaired with a paint brush. Now the *New Jersey* felt like a canoe and the roar of the storm was so great men could not hear their own voices. At noon, Halsey could not see the bow of his own ship. The sea dashed over the flight deck of the *Hancock* which was fifty-seven feet above the water line.

Ships rolled and pitched, creaked and clanked, and butted into the waves. As the storm increased, men wondered how they could possibly survive. They were at the mercy of the sea and the sea could be merciless. The circular storm blew north and south, east and west. Few were seasick. Fear was the magical antidote. Minds were too full of fright to think of such a trivial thing as seasickness. This was a matter of life and death.

Formations no longer existed as each captain fought to keep his own ship afloat. In the rolls and pitches, the smaller ships seemed as though they would break apart at any moment. How much could a ship take? How far could a ship roll and still right itself? The idea was to head into the wind. That was not so easy. And caught sideways, floods could ruin engines and all control would be lost.

The destroyers, waiting to be fueled, were low in ballast. Some took on salt water to gain stability. For one reason or another, some did not. Stability was the big problem and extra AA guns and radar equipment topside added to the problem. Men risked their lives to jettison everything possible that increased weight above. The captain of the *Dewey* was on the verge of ordering the mast cut down with an acetylene torch. It was unnecessary. The Number 1 stack crashed down at boat deck level and accomplished the same purpose of reducing "sail area."

The *Dewey* deck log described the horror:

1006. Captain ordered all port fuel tanks filled to capacity. 30,000 gallons of oil pumped to port side. Rolling through 40 to 50 degrees.

1020. Lost bridge steering control; steering aft. Telephone circuits began to go. Lost radio and TBS contact with rest of formation. . . . Wind and sea rising, barometer falling.

1102. Doctor reported many men had been injured by falling.

1130. Main engine stopped—main switchboard shorted from salt water. Secured main generator. Electrical power and lights all gone. 500 to 1,000 gallons of water entering #2 main forced draft intake on every big roll. Bucket brigade in mess hall and one aft kept water down.

1130. All control and communication lost from bridge. Dead in the water. The air . . . continually filled with salt spray 200 feet in the air or higher. Visibility zero. This blast of salt spray penetrated everything and grounded all electrical connections . . . 8 inches of water in all living spaces produced undesirable "free surface." All hands told to remain on port side. Rolling and pounding worse. Inclinometer to 73 degrees to starboard and stopped for a few seconds. Engine room (indicated) 75 degrees. The masts and stacks . . . swinging and expected to carry away at any time. Tops of 3 ready ammo lockers torn off and 80 pounds of 5 inch spilled over the side. . . . All thin shielding of ship stove-in by water on starboard side—by wind on port.

1145. The wind . . . estimated to be more than 110
knots. All hands performed in a commendable manner,
especially the engineers . . . no panic.

Surprisingly, the captain and crew of the *Dewey* survived
to tell the tale. Crews continually pumped and bailed while
others fought fires. Floods and fire, what could be worse?
Despite battening down, seas rushed down the hatches,
through the ventilators, into engine rooms, and caused short
circuits. Planes came loose, collided, and exploded.

The destroyer *Hickox* lost steering control because a flood
almost drowned the men who were trying to steer by hand
in the steering-engine compartment. With the vent systems
out, it was almost impossible to work in the engine room
more than a few minutes without collapsing. Lieutenant
Commander J. H. Wesson, the captain, saved the ship by
heaving to, lying dead in the water, and letting the ship find
her own way. Wesson said, "You cannot fight a typhoon."
His technique was an old sea trick during the days of
wooden ships. Luckily, it worked for the *Hickox*.

The *Monterey* caught fire when loose planes, like loose
cannons, skidded around the deck and broke into flames.
Eighteen aircraft burned on the hangar deck or were blown
over the side. Other carriers had similar troubles. And with
it all, the *Langley* rolled 70 degrees.

Destiny dealt harshly with some skippers and crews. For
some, the circumstances that preceded the typhoon were
critical. For others, perhaps it was simply timing. At exactly
the wrong moment their ships were in the wrong trough, or
the wind caught them at the wrong angle and it was all

over. Seamanship could only do so much in the hands of the furious gods.

The destroyer *Hull*, part of the oiler group screen, did not take on salt water ballast because her fuel tanks were seventy percent full. Lieutenant Commander James Marks had good reason to believe that was sufficient to ride out any storm. He was a young officer who had been through the worst North Atlantic tempests. Yet he had never run into such winds. Soon the *Hull* lost her way in the water, and rolls increased from 50 to 70 degrees. Then a gust of about one hundred ten knots put her on beam's end and she was gone. Only fifty-five of the ship's company of 264 were finally rescued.

Lieutenant Commander F. B. Garrett, captain of the destroyer *Monaghan*, found that he was unable to steer and attempts to ballast her weather side failed. She took several bad rolls and sank. Only six men survived. Garret was not among them.

Lieutenant Commander J. P. Andrea, captain of the *Spence*, had been in desperate need of fuel. He took on salt water too late, the rudder jammed, and after several deep rolls, she too went down with all except twenty-four men.

Oddly, the small destroyer escorts weathered the storm better. An officer of one DE later wrote that:

> "some men were doing their job in a matter of fact way—others were praying or sitting off by themselves, their faces white with fear. . . . We realized that we were in a typhoon and we knew we were on the wrong side of it—would pass through the center if we stayed afloat that long. . . . By 1300 we must have passed

through the center for there was a momentary lull—the seas hit us from all directions and the ship was racked and twisted—but she survived."

Their sharpest roll was 72 degrees, literally on her beam ends. At one bad moment, a powder case broke and sixty-pound projectiles rolled amid the powder. Less dangerous but more nerve-racking were the scratchy voices that came over the radio. It kept them on edge as they heard of the perils of others.

The DE *Tabberer* was thought to be a sure goner. When the sea calmed to some extent, no one sighted or heard from her. Finally a message reached Halsey telling of her plight. The *Tabberer*'s foremast had disappeared, and the radio and radar were destroyed. Nevertheless, she had not only won against the sea, she had deprived the sea of ten lost souls from the *Hull*. While other ships struggled to avoid foundering, Lieutenant Commander Henry L. Plage maneuvered his ship to take on the lucky survivors. His skill amazed hardened seamen. Plage's plan was to steam about fifty yards to windward of each man in the water and then drift toward him. While doing this, two cargo nets were tossed over the side along with several life rings on lines. Not only that, some of the better swimmers on board jumped into the sea with lines attached to them and helped the floundering men.

Halsey was so impressed he sent Plage a "well done for a sturdy performance" and awarded him a Legion of Merit.

Halsey assumed that Plage was an officer with long experience at sea. Such, he learned later, was not the case. Plage was a reserve officer from Atlanta who had been to sea only once before during an ROTC cruise while at Georgia Tech.

An organized air and sea search for survivors began as soon as possible and continued for the next four days. No one expected much success. How could anyone keep his head above that sea?

Tabberer was a part of the search on December 19 and her luck continued. She picked up twenty-eight more men. The crew of the *Tabberer* had no sleep for thirty-six hours, but when Halsey gave the order to search all night, the men gave a loud cheer. The miracles did not cease. They found a few more survivors that night and on the twentieth, they had the good fortune to rescue ten men on a raft from the *Spence.* Twice, sharks were so close to men in the water they had to be chased off with rifle fire. By the time the *Tabberer* finished, fifty-five men had been saved.

Other ships ran up rescue scores too. The DE *Swearer* found nine men from the *Spence,* and the destroyer *Brown* pulled twelve men from the *Hull* out of the ocean. All of the men who had been saved wore kapok jackets with whistles and flashlights and reflectors. None wore the more modern pneumatic kind of life preserver.

For all the good work, the lives saved were few compared with the lives lost. Seven hundred ninety men were never seen again. About fifteen of that number had been killed or washed overboard on ships that remained afloat. Three men were killed on the light carrier *Monterey.* More than eighty men suffered broken bones or worse injuries, and 146 planes were destroyed. It was a disaster. Admiral Nimitz said that the storm was "a more crippling blow to the Third Fleet

127

than it might be expected to suffer in anything less than a major action."

The typhoon had created such havoc that scheduled air strikes on Luzon were canceled and many ships went to Ulithi for repairs. But the war went on, and soon the strikes began again.

7.

Luzon

Japanese suicide planes menace the Third and
Seventh Fleets as American amphibious operations
begin at Lingayen Gulf in Luzon, the northernmost island of the Philippines.

Early in January, ships of the Seventh Fleet bombardment forces wove their way through the Philippines north
to Lingayen under the leadership of Admiral Oldendorf.
Lingayen Gulf, located north of Manila on Luzon, was the
next major landing area after Leyte. In support of the operation that kicked off the New Year, Halsey struck the
sources of enemy power in Formosa as well as Luzon. Sailing through the confined waters of the Philippines was a
risky business since the high nearby islands knocked out the
effectiveness of ship radar. Soon the advantage to the Japanese was clear.

Near Panay a twin-engine bomber came from out of no-
where to hit the escort carrier *Ommaney Bay*. It was almost
completely undetected until the crash. Fire flashed and explosions devastated the ship. Six of the survivors apparently
had a rendezvous with death. Picked up safely by other
ships, they were later killed by other kamikazes. This was
only the beginning. Before the end of the operation more
than fifty ships would be sunk.

The next day, two Zekes, just above the surface of the
water, evaded AA fire, climbed, turned, and crashed into

the *Manila Bay*. By sheer luck only two planes on the carrier caught fire and the damage control parties saved the ship. Still, casualties were high. Corpsmen came out again and again with their wire stretchers to carry off the dead and wounded. Morphine gave some momentary relief. Plasma and penicillin came to the aid of others.

Not all of the suicide pilots succeeded in reaching their targets. Many were brought down by interceptors or AA fire and died without achieving their cherished ambition. Nevertheless, their rate of damage was much higher than mere bombing and it had to be admitted that their fanatical courage was remarkable. Pilot after pilot aimed his plane at a ship and never wavered in his determination to end his life for the Empire. There was plenty of time for them to change their minds as they descended, but they sped toward their deaths without hesitation.

On January 6, Oldendorf's forces reached Lingayen Gulf for the preinvasion bombardment and the attacks continued undiminished. A flaming Japanese plane bashed the navigating bridge of the battleship *New Mexico* and the captain, communications officer, a British observer, and a *Time* correspondent were immediately killed.

Before the day ended, the destroyer *Long* was sunk and another destroyer, *Allen M. Sumner*, damaged. The situation was grim and would have been worse if the fast carriers had not bombed and strafed airfields that day. The Japanese had shuttled planes from Formosa for their weird attacks and it was estimated that there were still two hundred aircraft ready to do their worst on Luzon.

In the early evening more kamikazes came out. One hit the *California*. The kamikazes produced a devilish bonus

The damaged flight deck of the carrier *Sangamon* after it was struck by a kamikaze.

for their cause. Gun crews on board ships, in their anxiety to bring down the onrushing planes, became careless with their marksmanship, particularly when planes attacked at low level. The result was that "friendly" fire hit their own men and ships. Admiral Oldendorf minced no words. in warning all ships to be more careful.

Rear Admiral Theodore Chandler, the son of an admiral and grandson of a Secretary of the Navy, was on board the *Louisville* as commander of Crudiv (Cruiser division) 4. The *Louisville*, known as "Lady Lou" or "Man of War," had not been too lucky recently. She was hit for the second time as a suicide plane ripped through the bridge. Chandler, badly burned, helped with a fire hose and then waited his turn for medical help. By then it was too late. The fire had destroyed his lungs and he died.

The bombardment force carried on despite the increasing damage. Sailors in the gulf wondered why they did not receive more protection in the air. They saw few American planes. The apparent lack of support was deceptive. Actually, the interceptors were active miles away. They had to operate at a distance to make their interceptions effective.

The situation at Lingayen Gulf grew alarming. Hundreds of sailors had been killed and the amphibious assault had not even begun. There was no question of withdrawing, yet every sensible officer from Oldendorf on down wondered how much they could take. What would happen to the amphibious forces due in the gulf on the ninth? The thousands of troops packed in the transports and landing craft could be decimated if the rate of attack did not let up.

The assault forces, following the same route that Oldendorf had taken, began their long journey through the islands to reach Lingayen. En route, torpedoes headed toward the *Boise*, with General MacArthur on board, but forewarned by the *Phoenix*, the cruiser managed to avoid destruction. The attackers were two midget submarines. The little subs did not appear to be much bigger than torpedoes. Two brave men crammed themselves into the boat powered by storage batteries, which was little more than forty feet long and carried two torpedoes. The lives of both boat and crew were very short. This day, the destroyer *Taylor* rammed and sank one, while the other escaped to fight another day.

The suicide planes gave most of their attention to Oldendorf's heavy ships, but the amphibious forces were not totally ignored. They received a good share of harassment and more than their share of serious damage. The escort carriers, always an attractive target, came in for brutal punishment. The CVE *Kadashan Bay* was so badly damaged it had to return to Leyte. The transport *Callaway* with almost twelve hundred soldiers on board received a blow on the bridge that killed twenty-nine seamen, but did not touch a single soldier.

The attack forces arrived in the gulf as scheduled for the landings on January 9. The *Kitkun Bay*, another CVE, became one more of the wounded and she would be joined by others, but the intensity of the attacks lessened.

On D-Day, the troops began to disembark from the transports that filled the gulf. For once, many of the soldiers were glad to go ashore. They needed relief from the kamikazes and like good soldiers, they preferred the ground under their feet. Even a crowded transport had luxuries not found in a foxhole. Clean bunks, good food, and hot coffee were certainly more comfortable than the blood and sweat of jungle fighting. And yet the comforts combined with the dangers of the past few days had made the infantrymen restless to return to the things they understood better. They had been locked up too long.

As the small boats chugged toward the shore, the cruiser *Columbia* took her third hit in the forward main battery director. The *Columbia* was near the beach and unable to maneuver out of the way in the midst of the landing craft. Seconds later, a plane headed for Admiral Wilkinson's flagship, *Mount Olympus*, appeared ready to dive when it veered off under heavy antiaircraft fire. Perhaps the pilot was the exception to the rule and decided that suicide was not such a good idea. Or perhaps he was only a snooper. Whatever, the admiral sat calmly in his chair on the flag bridge and appeared totally unconcerned. Everyone else, sure that the end was near, was far less serene.

The Sixth Army found little opposition on the beaches because the Japanese, by plan, had retreated into the hills to make a stronger stand later. Before the infantrymen reached Manila they would run into many tough battles. At any rate, they had the luxury of a relatively easy landing.

During the night of the ninth, as suicide planes kept up their deadly work, the Japanese introduced a new form of suicide. It was the suicide boat. About seventy of them had been lying in wait in a concealed anchorage in the gulf. Their intent was to destroy the recently arrived shipping. At the same time, midget submarines helped them in their mission. If midget subs were not suicide boats, they were certainly the next best thing.

Ready to die for their cause, the suicide sailors moved stealthily among the amphibious ships during the dark night.

Before dawn arrived at least one transport and four LSTs were damaged and two LCIs were sunk. The mission was a one-way street and they did not come out a second night.

While the amphibious operations progressed, Halsey struck Formosa again to stem the wild air offensive and then steamed into the South China Sea. He hoped to find some of the remaining warships of the enemy fleet, especially *Ise* and *Hyuga*. He did not find the warships, but he found plenty of shipping and aircraft. Along four hundred miles of the Indo-China coast south to Saigon, he dealt harshly with the enemy. He also suffered losses. At Hong Kong, intense antiaircraft fire blackened the sky and brought down twenty-two planes. In eleven days the fast carriers traveled thirty-eight hundred miles in the South China Sea on their destructive mission and then took a crack at Formosa still again.

Formosa always put up strong resistance. Each time the task force raided the island they encountered trouble. Their visit this time was no different. Now that the Japanese were committed to suicide as a weapon of war, the action was worse. On January 20, TF38 destroyed more than a hundred planes on the island. They also took it on the chin with bomb hits on the *Langley* and a suicide crash on the *Ticonderoga*. The latter carrier fared the worst by far. Hundreds of men were added to the casualty list.

Shortly after the *Ticonderoga* was hit, a tricky Japanese pilot joined a returning flight of American planes. The scheme was not original, but it often worked because it fooled the radar operators. Over the *Maddox*, the pilot left the group and smashed into the destroyer. The ship remained afloat, but not without fatalities.

Carrier Strike Force

When the tired Fast Carrier Task Force returned to Ulithi near the end of January, Admiral Spruance, according to plan, relieved Admiral Halsey, and Mitscher relieved McCain.

When Halsey departed, he did so with the appreciative flair that made him so popular with the men under him. His message to the fleet said:

> I am so proud of you that no words can express my feelings. This has been a hard operation. At times you have been driven almost beyond endurance but only because the stakes were high, the enemy was as weary as you were, and the lives of many Americans could be spared in later offensives if we did our work well now. We have driven the enemy off the sea and back to his inner defenses. Superlatively well done. Halsey.

The Third Fleet was now the Fifth Fleet again, and TF38 became TF58. Spruance and Mitscher went to work to execute the big plans that they had worked on while Halsey and McCain had fought the enemy and roamed the seas.

8.

Iwo and Okinawa

The Japanese increase the intensity of their suicide
attacks during the American landings at Iwo Jima
in the Volcano Islands and Okinawa in the Ryukus.

Mitscher said, "He is probably more afraid of you than
you are of him." He was never given to heroic phrases, and
this was his way of reassuring his pilots that everything
would be all right. They were sixty miles off the coast of
Japan and anything could happen. It was harrowing to
realize that their next strikes would take them to Tokyo.

The mission was partly a diversion to distract the enemy
from the next landing at Iwo Jima, and partly to cut down
the Japanese ability to launch air attacks.

No Americans had struck the homeland from a carrier
since Jimmy Doolittle took off from the *Hornet* in 1942. For
all of its bravery and daring, that was a token raid and a
morale booster for the people back home that had little, if
any, effect upon the outcome of the war. Now TF58 arrived
with droves of planes to bomb war plants, crush air power,
and leave no doubt in the enemy mind about who was win-
ning the war.

Preparing planes for early morning takeoffs was a miserable job at best. Now, in February, the crews, accustomed
to tropical waters, contended with the foul, freezing weather
of the north. On a dark, cold morning there was little margin
for error working on the flight deck. A step or two in the

137

wrong direction, and a man could be cut to pieces by the whirling propellers. As always, however, the work went on regardless of risk and the aircraft roared off.

The Navy pilots did not find life any less easy with low ceilings, rain and snow squalls. For the first strike on Japan, the fighters, as usual, went first, then the bombers. They did not intend to annihilate urban populations with indiscriminate bombings. Instead, they looked for aircraft frame and engine plants in the Tokyo area.

Lieutenant Commander J. Bryan, a staff officer with Admiral Radford, a task group commander, listened to pilots in the ready room when they returned. The conversations had a casual tone that deceptively covered their tensions within or the exhilaration of a safe flight. With all the informality, the talk reflected a certain professionalism of men who knew their jobs.

One said, "I got some slugs in one, but I blacked out in the middle of it. I don't know what happened to him."

Another said, "I wasn't shooting at *him*, I was shooting at the plane. He must have had a spring in his chute, because it popped right open, and he was hanging in it, dead."

Still another, "Fujiyama was beautiful, but Tokyo looked like Hong Kong, only bigger and browner. It looked like part of the earth—reckon it was camouflaged? Anyhow, it's not like any city at home, no big buildings at all. All the reservoirs were frozen, and there was snow everywhere. I'd hate like hell to go down in that country."

And so it went. The conversations, no more heroic than Mitscher's, somehow instilled a sense of confidence. Perhaps because there was no affectation and no intention of being heroic. They had just accomplished one of the historic feats of the war and the conversations were just downright ordinary.

Some of the younger pilots, however, did not return. Mitscher had emphasized teamwork. In union there was strength. But the less experienced fighter pilots broke formation to engage in individual dogfights. Their eagerness was expensive. Sixty aircraft were lost.

In the afternoon, the destroyer *Haynesworth* sank three Japanese picket boats and then commenced to pick up those in the water who had survived their deadly shells. A number of the prisoners of war were transferred to the *Essex* where they received unusual treatment. No sadistic guards beat or tortured the captives. Instead, the curious carrier crew found the new arrivals a fascinating diversion from their daily routine. They gathered around the cells and gave the Japanese candy bars, cigarettes, and lessons in English, or at least English profanity. It was equally fascinating that the men on the *Essex*, at the forefront of the war, with their own lives at stake, were free of bitterness and personal belligerence.

Finally, poor weather forced Mitscher to call off the strikes and return to Iwo where Spruance and his compatriots, "Terrible" Turner and "Howling Mad" Smith were on hand for another amphibious landing. While the air attack on Japan was not a complete success because of weather, substantial damage had been inflicted without the loss of a single carrier.

Iwo Jima, in the Volcano Islands, was about six hundred miles south of Japan, and roughly six hundred miles north of Saipan. American strategists saw it as a valuable emergency landing area for the B-29s making bombing runs on

Japan. P-51 Mustangs could also take off from there to escort the longer-range bombers.

The volcanic island, once called Sulphur Island for the sulphur mines, was only five miles long and two-and-a-half miles wide. It was easily recognized from the sea by a dead volcano, 546 feet high at the southern end. That was Mount Suribachi. The unique beaches were a soft black which was ash, not sand.

The Japanese decided to make this little island a strong defense area. Like Peleliu, it had an underground system of tunnels and caves that could not be seen by reconnaissance planes. About twenty thousand men, under Lieutenant General Tadamichi Kuribayahi, were the island defenders. They dug in for dear life, but one older officer with more foresight than energy asked, "Why dig so many caves? We're all going to die anyway."

For weeks Iwo withstood heavy bombing from carrier planes and the Army Air Force. As the fanaticism of the kamikazes reached new heights, the operation of carriers in these waters was daring fate. Yoshi Miyagi, a kamikaze pilot, wrote, "I am nothing but a particle of iron attracted by a magnet—the American aircraft carrier." The prospects for an uneventful landing were not encouraging.

On D-Day, Hellcats dove in with five-inch rockets and 500-pound bombs, and Helldivers and Avengers followed with heavier bombs or napalm, a fire bomb. The napalm had a hideous purpose. It was meant to suck the oxygen out of the entrenchments. Many of them, however, failed to ignite.

By the time the carrier planes finished their runs, all the targets seemed to be eradicated. The invasion should be a pushover. Veterans of previous landings, however, knew that no one could ever overestimate the Japanese endurance and ability to withstand punishment. Hiding in their underground fortresses, they waited with every intention of defending their island to the last.

Once again, air power had shown its limits. The conquest of Iwo depended on the Marines fighting every step of the way. TF58 gave direct support with the help of Marine Corps artillery observers who would spot targets. Nevertheless, it was a bitter struggle with Marines taking terrible losses. The battle was immortalized by the famous photograph by Joe Rosenthal which showed the Marines raising the flag on Mount Suribachi. It was the most famous picture taken during the war. The sculptor Felix de Welden used the photograph as the basis for his bronze monument dedicated to the Marine Corps which stands at Arlington National Cemetery in the nation's capital.

The old *Saratoga* was one of the ships of TF58 that gave support off Iwo. The big ship, used in night operations, made a perfect target for a fifty-plane attack that had flown from the Bonin Islands one overcast day. Three bombs hit the carrier and then not one but four kamikazes crashed into her. Two hours later, another bomb hit.

Somehow, despite a big hole in the flight deck, a mixed-up pilot from a CVE landed on the *Saratoga* by mistake. As he got out of his plane, he said, "Gee I'm glad I'm not on that old *Sara*. All hell's broken loose out there!" One of the deck crew replied, "Take a good look around, brother. This *is* hell."

The same day, the escort carrier *Bismarck Sea* was sunk. The tough *Saratoga* remained afloat, but her fighting days were over when she returned to the United States.

The novelist John P. Marquand, serving as a war correspondent, was at Iwo. He was especially intrigued by the radio conversations in the background that came over the TBS (Talk Between Ships) on the bridge. The incessant words seemed to be ignored by everyone. It was true. Everyone disregarded the messages unless he was directly involved. The code words that he listened to and recorded made senseless sounds, and yet they went on and on.

"This is Peter Rabbit calling Audacity One—Peter Rabbit calling Audacity One—over . . . Audacity One calling Peter Rabbit . . . Come in, Peter Rabbit—over . . . Peter Rabbit to Audacity One—Shackle. Charley. Abel. Oboe. Noel Coward, Unshackle—over . . . Audacity One to Peter Rabbit—Continue as directed. Over . . . Peter Rabbit to Audacity One—Roger. Over . . ."

And so on and on.

The flawless diction in clear, unemotional tones made a deep impression upon Marquand. The words meant something to someone. He wondered who. It never stopped.

"Tiger Two is now in a position to give the stepchildren a drink. Will Audacity One please notify the stepchildren? . . . Bulldog calling Turtle. A pilot is in the water, southeast of Hot Rock. Pick him up. I repeat: in the water, southeast of Hot Rock. Pick him up . . ."

It was all so businesslike. Marquand wished he could learn the end of the story. What happened to the pilot? There was no way of telling. No one seemed to care. And yet someone did care very much.

Despite the losses at Iwo, especially the very heavy losses to the Marines, the operation was a success. Soon B-29s and P-51s had their base. TF58 now turned toward Japan again for more strikes, but bad weather interfered again and the task force returned to Ulithi for rest and repairs.

There was always a next campaign. The next campaign this time was Okinawa in the center of the 140-mile Ryuku chain of islands. The plan was to make Okinawa a staging area for the final assault against the Japanese mainland in the fall. It was only 340 miles south of Kyushu and could furnish airfields and anchorages for a large-scale invasion.

Although the Ryukus had been a part of Japan since the latter part of the nineteenth century, the people of these islands were a mixture of Chinese, Malayan, and Ainu and looked down upon as inferior by the Japanese. Densely populated, more than four hundred fifty thousand people, mostly farmers, lived in huts or small houses in the southern part of the island. The northern part was mountainous. For centuries an uneasy relationship had existed between the Okinawans and the Japanese, and yet the Okinawans were loyal to the Emperor.

At the doorstep of Japan, there was every reason to believe that the enemy air attacks would step up. The kamikazes were producing results for the Japanese and there were no signs that they would end their barbaric practice.

As the Japanese retreated from island to island, the wiser commanders realized that they were fighting a lost cause. The situation was hopeless, but there was no surrender. From island to island, the defenders were told that the Empire depended upon their valiant sacrifices.

At Okinawa, Japanese self-sacrifice reached a peak that

no Westerner could understand. The depth of feeling of the Orientals for their cause was like a bottomless well. Lives were gladly given for the good of the Emperor.

Surprisingly, there was not a complete shortage of enemy planes. Thousands of aircraft still remained. Throughout the war, production continued and many planes had actually improved in design. It was the shortage of trained pilots that had led to their acts of desperation. Training took time, and there was no time now.

The defense of Okinawa required massive suicide attacks far beyond any previous effort. Okinawa was now the "decisive battle for the defense of the homeland." Operation Ten-Go intended to destroy the amphibious forces from the sky.

On the ground, however, Okinawa defenses were not forgotten. Lieutenant General Mitsura Ushijima had about one hundred thousand men in his command. The 24th Division of fourteen thousand men had come from Manchuria, the twelve thousand men of the 62nd Division were veterans of fighting in China, and there was the 44th Independent Mixed Brigade of five thousand men. That was not all. There were artillery units, service and labor troops, a home guard, and a tank regiment. Thousands of sailors would fight on land and seven hundred fifty high school students formed a dedicated body called "Blood and Iron for the Emperor" for guerrilla warfare.

Ushijima concentrated his defense in the south in rugged country that lent itself well to the Japanese techniques of caves and tunnels. Peleliu and Iwo may have been losing battles, but the caves served well against air strikes and offshore bombardment. They were also costly for the advancing troops.

Lieutenant General Simon Bolivar Buckner, Jr., the son of a Confederate general, was the Commanding General of the American Expeditionary Force that would lead both Army and Marine divisions against this Japanese bastion. Admiral Spruance, as commander of the Fifth Fleet, was in overall command of the naval forces of about fifteen hundred ships. D-Day, scheduled for Easter Sunday, was April 1, 1945.

Mitscher's job of reducing enemy air power meant more strikes against the homeland. In March, he took the Fast Carrier Task Force north for an attack on the airfields of Kyushu, the southernmost major island of Japan.

On March 18, the first carrier strike swept over forty-five airfields on Kyushu. The grand sweep should have created havoc. It did not match expectations because pilots found few planes on the ground. The Japanese had been forewarned by a sighting report and took off to escape attack on the ground. Some planes flew north to protect themselves. Others took off to hammer away at TF58. The carriers received a hot reception that differed from their last visit.

The old *Enterprise*, still battling as she had at the start of the war, was the first carrier hit. The bomb turned out to be a dud, but the dud killed one man and wounded two others. The *Intrepid*, another scarred veteran, shot down a twin-engine Betty that blew up at such close range, two men were killed and many wounded. The *Yorktown* was next. Three Judys dropped bombs. Two missed; the third hit the signal bridge, went through one deck, and killed five men. The casualties were relatively low and the damage was not too severe. Still any carrier crewman could see that they could easily become sitting ducks so close to the mainland.

The next day, TF58 attacked shipping in the Inland Sea. Search planes had sighted some familiar warships the day before and they could not be passed up. Old acquaintances such as the giant *Yamato*, the battleship/carriers *Hyuga* and *Ise*, and carriers *Amagi*, *Katsuragi*, and *Ryuho* were stationary targets. Squadrons hit sixteen ships, but none were sunk and the damage was of little consequence.

During these March strikes, Lieutenant (j.g.) Ronald Lee Somerville, a dive-bomber pilot from the *Hancock*, had some mechanical difficulties and made a forced landing in the middle of Kagoshima Bay, fifteen miles from the mouth. Almost at once, two reliable Kingfishers, the unsung heroes of the war, catapulted from the *Astoria* with an escort of twenty-four fighters. On the way to the rescue, a squadron of Japanese fighters intercepted them. Although five Japanese planes were shot down, Ensign David Kelleher's plane from the *Cabot* was hit and he parachuted into the bay. As luck would have it, he landed near Somerville. With the attackers discouraged, the Kingfishers landed about two miles off the beach of a major airfield and picked up the two men. Within the hour everyone was back safe and sound.

TF58 had not finished taking heavy blows. Early one morning, just after the sun had risen, an undetected plane dropped a bomb on the *Wasp* that exploded aircraft in the hangar deck, passed through the crew quarters on Number

2 deck, and then reached Number 3 deck where cooks and mess attendants, preparing breakfast, were massacred. The single bomb started fires on five decks, six water mains broke, and the high octane aviation gasoline streamed down to the lower decks. With 370 men killed or wounded, the men of the *Wasp* showed their mettle and fought the fires with the utmost skill. Within fifteen minutes the fires were out and soon the *Wasp* started to recover planes again. Then a kamikaze, undoubtedly hoping to put an end to the carrier, came in for the kill. He was disappointed in his last dream when he missed by what seemed like inches.

While the *Wasp* fought valiantly, the *Franklin*, known as "Big Ben," ran into a worse hell. Another undetected plane dropped two bombs. The first blew up on the hangar deck, destroyed the forward elevator, and spread fires throughout the hangar and Number 3 deck. The armed planes, ready for strikes, went off and devastated the area. The second enemy bomb hit the flight deck. Fire and smoke enveloped the entire ship.

Captain Leslie Gehres, on the bridge, was knocked down by the first explosion. When he got up, he saw the fire on the starboard side forward and ordered full right rudder to keep the wind away from the planes aft. Then he learned that the after part of the ship was in flames too. He swung the ship to port to bring the wind to the starboard beam and slowed down to two-thirds speed.

The explosions went on and on in series. The bombs in one plane set off bombs in another. Mitscher, miles away on the *Bunker Hill*, heard the violent blasts.

Some of the fighter bombers were armed with "Tiny Tim" rockets and they went off too. Commander Joe Taylor, the executive officer, said, "Some screamed by to starboard, some to port, and some straight up the flight deck." The weird whooshing, he thought, was one of the worst spectacles that anyone could witness. Some went straight up, and others tumbled end over end. Instinctively, the firefighting crews hit the deck every time one took off on its deadly run.

As the fire swept through the decks, all the ready ammunition in the lockers and gun mounts astern of the island exploded. Orders were given to flood the ammunition storage, but the system did not function and the after magazine was not flooded. The one lucky break of that horrible day occurred when, quite irrationally, it failed to explode.

The *Franklin* was the flagship of Admiral R. E. Davison, commander of Task Group 58.2. He ordered the cruiser *Santa Fe* to help the *Franklin* and then transferred his flag and staff to the *Hancock*. As Davison left, he suggested to the captain that he issue the order to prepare to abandon ship. Gehres, a stubborn man, answered that he thought he could save the ship. How anyone could have such thoughts in the midst of this holocaust is hard to imagine.

Hundreds were now dead on the decks. Hundreds of others were dying. When it was possible to pass the word, Gehres ordered everyone except key officers and men to abandon ship. Destroyers picked dozens of men out of the sea while the *Santa Fe* took on 833 men, including all of the wounded. The cruiser faithfully remained alongside the stricken carrier for a dangerous three hours.

Little doubt existed that the ship should be abandoned, but Gehres, talking over the TBS, said to Mitscher, "This is the commanding officer of the *Franklin*. You save us from

A Japanese Judy falls in flames after being hit by
antiaircraft fire from the carrier *Wasp*.

The burning and damaged *Princeton* hit by a Japanese dive bomber.

the Japs and we'll save this ship." Mitscher watched the black smoke rising in the distance. It looked ominous and yet he had faith in Gehres. He replied, "You tell him we'll save him." Mitscher had the *Wasp* as well as the *Franklin* to worry about and he covered both.

The *Franklin* had been hit at 0708. By about 1000, crews evacuated fire and engine rooms, and the ship was dead in the water. Damage control parties remaining on the ship could be blown up at any minute or trapped in flames. With stamina and courage that was indescribable, they persevered without any thought of themselves. Lieutenant (j.g.) Donald Gary, working his way through the ship, discovered three hundred men trapped in a dark mess compartment and led them through the dense smoke to safety. By noon, the situation was more or less in hand. Things were not good, but the ship's list had stabilized at 13 degrees.

At 1254, a Judy appeared to finish off the crippled ship. The bombing run missed. Although the *Franklin* was only fifty-five miles off the coast of Japan, the enemy was unable or unwilling to pursue the ship.

The cruiser *Pittsburgh* took *Franklin* in tow and they slowly sailed south. Explosions still continued and destroyers came alongside from time to time to spray water on recurring fires.

During the night, one of the fire rooms started to work again and the next day, three of the eight boilers were lighted. This gave the ship a speed of two knots and allowed the *Pittsburgh* to tow at six knots. The list made towing difficult and attempts to counter-flood got out of hand. The carrier rolled to port and stayed there with a list of about

151

10 degrees. On the twentieth, bridge steering began again and a portable radio was set up on the bridge. By noon, with four boilers working, the speed stepped up to a fast fourteen knots. A half-hour later, the tow was cast off and the *Franklin* proceeded at her own speed.

About four hundred men worked the ship and another two hundred remained on board. By March 24, the gallant ship reached Ulithi. Later, she would sail to New York City via Pearl Harbor, a distance of twelve thousand miles. No capital ship in the history of the Navy had ever taken such a beating and survived. And yet, the casualties were heavy with 832 dead and 270 wounded.

Despite the ghastly distractions, TF58 did not let down on their strikes against Japan. Before they finished, they claimed that the Japanese had lost 482 planes in the air and on the ground. On March 21, the fast carriers turned south again to give close support for the Okinawa landing.

Officially, the day for landing at Okinawa, Operation Iceberg, was called L-Day, and "L" stood for "Love." It was Easter Sunday and the spirit of love did not seem apparent on the surface. But the thoughts of most men that day must have been of loved ones at home.

Happily, the initial landing was easy. There was no opposition on the beaches and the troops quickly moved inland. The struggles of the infantrymen were still to come.

The Navy, however, bore the brunt of early attacks. If kamikazes had caused trouble before, it was nothing compared with the onslaught at Okinawa.

Operation Ten-Go planned on forty-five hundred conventional and suicide planes to stop the Americans. Their goal was too ambitious. They could only organize about 355 suicide planes and 344 conventional planes, but that was enough to cause consternation off Okinawa's shores.

Some admirals seemed to have nine lives. Still, they were no more immune from these mad attacks than anyone else. The day before the landing, a kamikaze crashed Admiral Spruance's flagship *Indianapolis.* Spruance was not hurt, but he had to transfer his flag and staff to the battleship *New Mexico.*

The first of ten mass air attacks began on the afternoon of April 6. The Japanese dispatched 230 Navy planes and 125 Army planes to smash into the United States fleet. Another 341 aircraft pursued shipping with conventional tactics.

The destroyers protecting the landing craft at radar picket stations on the outer perimeter were the choice targets. None of the ships, however, were really neglected. Closer to the beaches transports and heavy combat vessels received their share of grief too. By the end of the day, nineteen ships had been sunk or damaged, and the loss of life was staggering. Probably half of the attacking planes were shot down by the combat air patrol or antiaircraft fire. The remainder did the destruction.

The Japanese had another suicide mission in mind. The great *Yamato* escaped in previous engagements. Now, she set forth from the Inland Sea with a crew of 2,767. A light cruiser and eight destroyers accompanied the big battleship without any air support.

Admiral Toyoda, commander of the Combined Fleet, had no illusions when he issued his ingenious order to Vice Admiral Seichi Ito. "I knew very well," he said later, "what the fate of warships would be without air cover, and that the probability of success was very slight. Nevertheless, we had to do everything to help our troops at Okinawa."

Toyoda called the force a "Surface Special Attack Unit." He told his commanders that the plan was "for a breakthrough operation of unrivaled bravery so that the power of the Imperial Navy may be felt in this one action in order that the brilliant tradition of the Imperial Navy's surface forces may be exalted and our glory handed down to posterity."

Each ship had only enough fuel for a one-way trip. This did not seem to disturb the crews. They appeared at ease and the night before they left there were several joyous farewell parties.

When Tameichi Hara, captain of the cruiser *Yahagi*, toured his ill-fated ship, he saw men sleeping peacefully in their hammocks. Hara himself felt a sense of joy and when he went above he cried out, "Nippon banzai, Nippon banzai."

Submarines sighted this enemy force on April 7. Spruance preferred a surface engagement, but Mitscher was desperately anxious to show what his aircraft could do to this gigantic battleship. It was the old debate between airmen and seamen about air power versus sea power that had gone on since the 1920s. Mitscher had a chance to show his stuff and let the world know that the fast carriers had become the premier ships of the Navy. *Yamato*'s sister ship, *Musashi*, had gone down in the battle of Leyte Gulf, but it was never clear whether the credit should have gone to aircraft or submarines.

Mitscher told his chief of staff, "Inform Admiral Spruance that I propose to attack the *Yamato* sortie group at 1200 unless otherwise directed." Mitscher's message to Spruance read, "Will you take them or shall I?" Spruance replied, "You take them."

Mitscher launched a strike of 280 aircraft to seek and destroy the enemy force. Shortly after noon, the battle began. Wave after wave of planes zoomed in on the last great remnant of the Japanese Imperial Fleet. The ships threw up antiaircraft fire with little effect. Two bombs hit the *Yamato* mainmast, two minutes later a torpedo found its target. Within the first hour three more torpedoes broke open the port side. More bombs hit, then more torpedoes. When the outcome was certain, Admiral Ito formally shook hands with his staff and retired to his cabin to await the end. The ship's captain gave orders to a seaman to lash him to the compass. He wanted to be sure to go down with his ship. By 1423, the monstrous ship sank with almost twenty-five hundred men. Only 269 of the crew survived.

Yamato was not the only ship to go down. The light cruiser and a destroyer sank, three severely damaged destroyers were eventually scuttled, and the remaining four destroyers were damaged.

Lieutenant (j.g.) W. E. Delaney, an Avenger pilot, ended up in the water after he had made a low-level attack on the *Yamato*. The explosion from his bomb hit set his plane on fire and he and his crewmen had to bail out. The crewmen drowned in their parachute jump, but Delaney was able to get into his rubber raft and watch the *Yamato* go down. He found himself in the middle of Japanese survivors swimming around him. Two big PBM seaplanes spotted Delaney and one landed amid the Japanese, picked up Delaney, and returned him safely.

Meanwhile, the suicide air attacks at Okinawa continued. One morning Mitscher sent four aircraft piloted by Marines to serve as sentinels about a hundred miles north of the task force to forward advance information. Bad weather set in after they had departed and the pilots were reported missing. In the afternoon search planes had no success in finding them.

Mitscher said to Jimmy Flatley, his operations officer, "Get me a chart and a pair of dividers." Mitscher measured the distance on the chart and said, "Those pilots are right here." He pointed to a spot hundreds of miles away from the task force. "Send a message to the submarines to pick them up." Flatley was skeptical, but he did as he was ordered and a submarine picked up the Marines.

Mitscher's fine touch was based upon his depth of knowledge and attention to detail. He had concluded that the Marines thought they were flying in a fifty-mile wind and he estimated from later aerology information that they were up against a hundred-mile wind and had run out of gas because they did not know the true wind speed. No wonder men had confidence in him. His humility never hid his skill.

Ashore, intense resistance gave infantrymen one rough challenge after another. At one time they reached the top of a hill only to find that an inaccessible cave on the other side could not be destroyed. It had cost three hundred casualties. The Army, willing to accept the hazard, asked for carrier planes to bomb the cave entrance with American troops only fifty yards away.

Fighter pilots rehearsed the run, realizing all too well the risks, studied the photographs, and then struck at an altitude that was hardly above hilltop. Their amazing accuracy accomplished the mission without scathing a soldier. No one could surpass the United States Navy in precision bombing.

Destroyers on picket duty took terrible beatings from the air attacks. At times the crews felt like they were on their own suicide missions as one destroyer after another was hit. Wounded ships often went to the aid of others worse off than themselves. Frequently it meant sailing into an area undergoing multiple suicide dives. Acts of heroism became an everyday affair.

The Japanese ingenuity for self-destruction knew no bounds. Now another way to die for the Emperor went into action at Okinawa. Americans called it the "baka" bomb. "Baka" in a rough translation of Japanese meant "screwball." The weapon was a 4,700-pound bomb with rocket propulsion and a pilot. Cast off from a Betty bomber, the mother plane, it could reach a diving speed of 600 miles per hour. It was a small target, only twenty feet long with a wing span of sixteen-and-a-half feet, which made it very difficult to shoot down.

The first destroyer sunk by the baka was the *Mannert L. Abele*. A Zeke hit the *Abele* first, and the baka came next. The ship went down in five minutes.

In April, another Friday the thirteenth came up on the calendar. Men were still reeling from a major air attack the previous day when a somber announcement came over loudspeakers on ships throughout the fleet. "Attention. Attention. All hands. President Roosevelt is dead. Repeat, our Supreme Commander, President Roosevelt is dead."

The news was unexpected and unbelievable. Many sailors had seen the President at Pearl Harbor a few months before and he had looked tan and fit. Shocked officers and men felt a personal loss, as though a close friend had gone. The sentiment was deep and real and, regardless of political beliefs, universal. No one had realized until then how closely they had associated themselves with the President. His image had become so strong over the years that he seemed like an intimate friend. The younger men could scarcely remember anyone else in the White House. Now, the confident war leader who had given strength in the darkest hours had left them.

Two days later, on every ship in the fleet, chaplains or commanding officers conducted memorial services for the President. The enemy could wait while they paid their respects.

Under a new, little-known President, the war went on with the same determination. Throughout April, the Fifth Fleet fought off attack after attack. Some days were worse than others. On April 16, the destroyer *Laffey* set some sort of a record by fighting twenty-two separate air attacks. The ship was hit by six kamikazes, four bombs, strafing, and near-misses, and surprisingly survived.

To the south of Okinawa, off a group of islands called Sakishima Gunto, TF58 received help from a new carrier force. It was designated TF57. American commanders had looked upon this help with a certain amount of suspicion. In the beginning, at least, there was an instinctive feeling that this new-found support might cause more trouble than it was worth. With the growth of the fast carriers, many felt the new force was simply unwanted and unneeded. There was also more than a little nationalistic spirit at stake. The Pacific war was an American war, or perhaps more accurately, an American, Australian, New Zealander war. Now strangers came into their midst in the final days, rather than the early days when they would have been welcomed with open arms.

TF57 was a British Carrier Force under Vice Admiral Sir H. B. Rawlings, RN. After the fall of Singapore, the British had almost disappeared. Were they here now for political reasons? Would they only create friction with their different methods? Happily, the small chip on American shoulders soon disappeared. The British meshed in smoothly under the intelligent leadership of Rawlings and Rear Admiral Sir Philip L. Vian, RN, commander of the First Aircraft Squadron who were well-seasoned combat veterans in other waters. More important, as the number of damaged American ships increased, the British served a very useful purpose.

No one could deny that the British added a romantic touch with the bold names of their carriers, HMS *Indomitable, Victorious, Illustrious, Indefatigable,* and *Formidable.* And they lived up to their names.

The British carriers had one advantage. Their flight decks, unlike those on the American ships, were well-armored with thick steel that did a better job of withstanding kamikazes. Nevertheless, they were not immune. *Indomitable, Illustrious,* and *Indefatigable* took severe blows.

The mounting list of damages and casualties from the kamikazes concerned everyone, but no one believed that they would influence the final outcome of the war. The ground battle advanced and in time one more island would be taken. With experience, combat air patrols improved their defensive techniques and in any tally the Japanese were bound to end up on the losing end.

Such logical thinking, however, did little to help the men who had to live through this nightmare. Taut nerves, knotted stomachs, sleepless nights, and the anticipation, always the anticipation, became a part of their lives.

During April, about four hundred kamikazes hit TF58. Fighters splashed about 233 suiciders, and antiaircraft fire knocked down another ninety. Nevertheless, during the same period, twenty-four ships were sunk, one hundred severely damaged, and 120 ships received "minor" damage.

In May there was no let-up. The fast carriers had escaped the brutal treatment that the destroyers had taken in April. Then the relative quiet changed for them in May.

Gruesome scenes on crashed ships were repeated over and over again. The blood spilling, horrible burns, the dead and dying, all had a deep psychological effect upon those lucky enough to remain physically unharmed. Stories abounded throughout the fleet of men who narrowly escaped death. The living were often shocked to be alive. They asked themselves if it was destiny. Slight alterations in a routine day, or a step here instead of a step there, often meant the difference between living and dying. Someone unwittingly taking a minute or two less on a task might find that that was the reason he was alive. Or for the same reason, someone else might have died. It was nerve-racking to say the least. Simple movements took on tremendous meaning and the lucky ones wondered how long their luck would hold. When would their time come? It was like trying to stay on a rolling log in the water.

On May 11, Mitscher's flagship, *Bunker Hill*, had been at sea for fifty-nine consecutive days. Since the fall of 1943, the carrier had been in every major air strike and amphibious landing and had earned eleven battle stars. About ten o'clock in the morning, the Combat Information Center (CIC) reported to the bridge that a close support air group returning to the ship might be a cover for some enemy planes tagging along. It was not possible to say for sure, and the clouds did not help.

The CIC hunch was right. A couple of minutes later, a Zeke dropped a 500-pound bomb on the flight deck, which passed through the side of the ship and exploded above water. About the same time, a kamikaze dove into the middle of fighters armed for takeoff and slid across the deck as gas tanks exploded.

Another enemy plane appeared, climbed steeply, turned, and plunged into the *Bunker Hill*. The released bomb hit amidships and went off in the gallery deck where a number of Mitscher's staff worked. The plane hurtled into the island less than a hundred feet from the admiral. He stepped out on the starboard side of the flag bridge, saw the wreckage and the fire shooting upward and did not say a word. His own sea cabin was in ruins.

In the fighter squadron ready room, pilots waited for their orders. An instant later, most of them were dead from suffocation.

Smoke poured into the flag plot through the door and ventilators and Arleigh Burke ordered everyone out. The room was so thick with smoke one officer got out by following the edge of the chart table.

In the meantime, gunners shot down a third kamikaze aimed at the ship. Explosions blew or forced three hundred men to jump overboard.

Mitscher watched the fire and heard the screams of dying

161

men. Counting the heads of his own staff, he learned that thirteen had been killed. Deeply depressed, Mitscher refused to discuss the deaths then or later. It hurt too much. Until now he had projected an invincible front, but the front was beginning to wear thin.

Mitscher knew that he had to shift his flag and staff to another ship. He temporarily transferred his command to Admiral Sherman, one of the task group commanders on the *Essex*, and prepared to leave. The *Bunker Hill* did not sink, but the savage destruction cost 389 lives and 264 wounded.

Mitscher reestablished his command on the *Enterprise*. The "Big E" now had outdone all other carriers with twenty battle stars. Along the way she had taken plenty of punishment, and already two kamikazes had hit her. But she was still in the war.

Three days after Mitscher had left the *Bunker Hill*, twenty-six planes attacked the fleet. All but one were shot down. That one struck the *Enterprise*. In the explosion, Mitscher remained standing while everyone around him hit the deck. He never flinched and some people thought his nerve control was inhuman. Without raising his voice, Mitscher said, "Flatley, tell my task group commanders that if the Japs keep this up they're going to grow hair on my head yet." The joke broke the tension and everyone who could went back to work again. This time six of the staff were wounded.

The suicide plane had crashed through the forward elevator and the bomb went off five decks below. Columns of gray and white smoke rose hundreds of feet in the air and fires spread through the forward end of the hangar. The

Dense smoke mushrooms up from the deck of the *Enterprise*
after it was struck by a Japanese kamikaze off Okinawa.

man who knocked out the *Enterprise* was Chief Pilot Tomi Zai. Unlike many kamikazes, he did not die unknown. His calling cards were found in the wreckage.

In a frantic seventeen minutes, the firefighters had the situation under control and in a half-hour the fire was out. Nevertheless, the *Enterprise*, veteran of so many hard experiences, had seen the end of her fighting days. She returned home with a proud war record that had been built since the black days of Pearl Harbor. In her active wartime career, she had run up a remarkable score of sinking seventy-one ships and 911 aircraft.

Within a few days, Halsey and McCain relieved Spruance and Mitscher in the normal course of scheduled events. Mitscher would not return to the Pacific again, but when he left the men of the task force knew that he was the man who had taken the fast carriers from the Marshalls to Japan and had molded them into one of the most respected outfits in the Navy. He would die shortly after the war, an exhausted man who had served his country well.

For the past two-and-a-half months the fast carriers had taken special risks to defend Okinawa. Mitscher emphasized in his report that the task force had "operated daily in a 60 mile square area East of Okinawa less than 350 miles from Kyushu."

At the end of May, Admiral Sherman took his task group to Leyte Gulf for a rest after seventy-nine days of sustained operation at sea. He calculated that his flagship *Essex* sailed 33,865 miles in that time and that the gunners had fired more than two thousand rounds of five-inch ammunition, sixteen thousand rounds of 40mm, and fourteen thousand rounds of 20mm. His air group flew 6,460 sorties, dropped

Iwo and Okinawa

1,041 tons of bombs, and shot more than a million rounds of ammunition. The expenditure of this destruction led to sinking seventeen ships, damaging fifty-seven ships, shooting down 220 planes, and destroying eighty-seven aircraft on the ground. On the debit side, he lost thirty planes in combat.

Fast carrier crews remained off Okinawa for another month and it was an assignment that they did not enjoy. They wanted offensive, not defensive duty. Halsey and McCain disliked being tied down as much as Spruance and Mitscher.

McCain wrote that staying close to Okinawa "is wasteful of force and fails to exploit the fast carrier assets of mobility, surprise, and concentration. It invites damage to the fast carriers and divests them from profitable targets which only they can reach."

Few people disagreed with McCain's sentiments. The defensive stand at Okinawa was a nasty and costly assignment. It was, however, a necessity and the fast carriers fulfilled their unpleasant duty nobly. The carriers had been immobilized because the Japanese ground forces had put up a strong resistance which prevented the American Army from taking airfields. The Army had also been unable to install enough radar so that patrols and picket boats could end their dangerous sentinel duty.

When Halsey asked Spruance how the southwest Pacific Army Air Force based in the Philippines was doing, Spruance replied sarcastically, "They've destroyed a great many sugar mills, railroad trains, and other equipment." Halsey sputtered, "Sugar mills can't damage our fleet! Why the hell don't they destroy their planes?"

The admirals were undoubtedly prejudiced, but the Army Air Force did not subscribe to the precision bombing attacks in the Navy manner. It was a matter of philosophy, background, and training. In the meantime, the Navy accepted daily risks to protect the Army.

By the end of the Okinawa campaign, the Navy had thirty ships sunk, 368 ships damaged, and 763 planes lost. Almost ten thousand sailors were casualties and about half of that number were killed. It was the heaviest loss of any naval operation in the war. It was no less easy for the Army. Among the troops, 7,613 men were killed, including General Buckner.

Halsey wasted little time in making plans to strike Japan. The Okinawa operation was winding down and he had the opportunity to free his ships and planes for more aggresive action.

9.

Victory

Planes from fast carriers strike the Japanese homeland with all their might.

No sooner had Halsey taken command of the Third Fleet than the winds began to roar. It was typhoon trouble again. And again confusion and uncertainty surrounded the forecasts and proper course to weather the storm. With one eye on Okinawa and another on Kyushu, many miles separated Radford's northernmost group of carriers and Clark's southernmost group.

First signs of the storm appeared on June 1 when Weather Control at Guam saw a threatening formation north of the Palau Islands. For the next three days, however, there were no definite reports. Delay and indecision, understandable or not, only made the situation worse.

Halsey, anxious to avoid another false prediction, studied all the available information carefully. The latest charts, tracks, and dispatches came to his immediate attention. And yet, when it was all added up, a clear picture was missing.

The wind and sea grew stronger from the southeast, but no one could confidently forecast what would happen. The typhoon, like the one in December, was so small that it was difficult to trace and the scattered ships of the Third Fleet reported different conditions. "Jocko" Clark ran into rough weather while Radford did not find too much to worry about.

Early on the morning of June 5, Clark sent McCain a message that read, "I can get clear of the center of the storm quickly by steering 120 degrees. Please advise." This baffled McCain. He replied, "We have nothing on our scope to indicate storm center." The irritated Clark, buffeted about by the mounting sea, responded, "We very definitely have. We have had one for one and a half hours."

McCain did not change the course, but a little later he asked Clark for more information. After receiving Clark's report, McCain still maintained the same course but gave Clark permission to use his own judgment. It was a long night. The time was then 0440.

Clark's suggested course of 120 degrees at 0420 would have taken him clear. By the time McCain freed him to do as he saw fit it was too late.

Soon the barometer fell to 28.98 and the wind blew in gusts up to ninety knots. Clark tried a number of courses to find a more comfortable condition. At 0519, near the storm center, he radioed McCain, "We are maneuvering to find the best course, should be out soon. The wind is now eighty knots."

Nearby, the destroyer *Maddox* rolled 60 degrees. In less than an hour, gusts of wind ripped up to a hundred knots, and the visibility ranged from zero to one mile.

The cruiser *Pittsburgh*, plowing through the mountainous waves, lost a plane on her port catapult. When it blew off, a fire started in the anchor windlass room. The fire was extinguished without too much trouble, but the captain sensed that there was worse to come. In a few minutes, Captain Gingrich ordered Condition 1. Everything was battened down and watertight areas locked up. In another three minutes, he ordered Condition Z. This made the enlisted men in the forward compartments get out of their bunks, where they probably felt safer, and go to their battle stations. The captain's order could not have been more timely if he had looked into a crystal ball. Fifteen minutes later, the ship ran into two monstrous waves that sheared off 104 feet of the steel bow as though it was a piece of paper. The bow sailed away on its own and became one more hazard of the sea. The watertight bulkheads held and the *Pittsburgh* continued to fight its way through the sea without its bow. Gingrich showed his skill as a seaman by eventually reaching Guam for repairs.

Almost all of the ships in Clark's group received some kind of damage. Near the eye of the storm they faced winds of maximum intensity. At 0700, Clark reached the center and for a few minutes there was an eerie dead calm. Then the howling whirlwinds began again and the ships battled the storm for another five hours. The flight decks of the *Hornet* and *Bennington* were now worthless. Twenty-five feet of their decks caved in and the *Bennington* lost six planes. A seaman on a catwalk of the *Belleau Wood* was washed overboard and a large number of aircraft were destroyed.

The destroyers fared better than in the previous typhoon and none were lost. Although the two typhoons were similar, the second did not last as long. As it was, the damage was more than enough. Six men were killed and others were seriously hurt.

The storm did not distract the task force from its mission. In another day or two they attacked again. But the Navy never forgets such incidents. A court of inquiry severely criticized Halsey for the losses in two typhoons. Halsey, however, was a man who believed in taking his own part. He replied that the "law of storms" can allow a single ship to make a last-minute evasion of the center force, but it was almost impossible for fleets that stretched out for miles. He reminded his critics that typhoons were erratic and frequently could not be predicted because of insufficient weather reports. Finally, he emphasized a fact that no one had given any attention. "Forces under my command," he wrote, "avoided no less than eleven typhoons without damage during extended operations in the typhoon belt." The matter dropped.

Halsey turned again to Japan. Targets on the southern island, Kyushu, became fewer and fewer and the task force steamed north off Honshu. There they found that the Japanese had cleverly camouflaged their aircraft and it was much more difficult to find something to strafe.

Early in July, Halsey received a strange top-secret message from Washington. He was ordered not to attack Kikura, Nigata, Kyoto, or Hiroshima in southern Japan. No reason was given. Halsey moved the force north again. This time he was beyond the range of the Army Air Force B-29s that had been pounding urban areas.

In northern Honshu and Hokkaido, the northernmost of the main islands, the key target destroyed was the Aamori-Hakodate ferry line that carried about thirty percent of the coal between Hokkaido and Honshu. While making air strikes, the heavy battleships and cruisers moved closer to the coast and bombarded industrial plants.

As Japan grew ever weaker, the carriers returned to the Tokyo area, and then, toward the end of July, struck Kure,

Kobe, and other ports on the Inland Sea. Some of the ir-repressible warships of the Imperial Fleet lingered on and Halsey intended to leave no stone unturned. The battle-ship *Haruna*, which had been reported sunk in the first days of the war was finally sent to the bottom. Along with her went, among others, the *Hyuga*, and *Ise* which up to then must have been the luckiest ships in the fleet. They had made one narrow escape after another.

Halsey said in his usual bombastic way, "What is left of the Japanese Navy is helpless, but just for luck, we're going to hunt them out of their holes. The Third Fleet's job is to hit the Empire hard and often. We are doing just that, and my only regret is that our ships don't have wheels so that when we drive the Japs from the coast, we can chase them inland."

The war was in its final days. And yet, danger was al-ways present. Lieutenant Commander Richard Crommelin, one of five brothers in the Navy who had survived all kinds of trouble, was killed in an air collision during an air strike. Sporadic attacks of kamikazes, and occasional spurts of effort by conventional fighters, were continually breaking out. Far away, on July 28, en route from Guam to Leyte, the cruiser *Indianapolis* that had served as Admiral Spru-ance's flagship, was sunk by a submarine with the loss of hundreds of men. Early in August, Admiral Nimitz ordered TF38 to strike a nest of enemy aircraft in northern Honshu. It was a wise decision. The Japanese Navy had collected two hundred bombers with the intention of crash landing two thousand suicide troops on major B-29 bases in the Marianas.

No one could let his guard down. As far as most people

171

Under the wing of a United States Navy bomber bombs can be seen falling on a Japanese aircraft carrier.

knew, the war was a long way from over. One of the favorite phrases of sailors during that summer of 1945 was, "The Golden Gate in '48." It was their pessimistic view of when the war would end.

The prevalent military thought was that Japan would only be conquered by invasion. The Japanese had already shown that they could fight on bitterly to the last man. A top secret plan, "Olympic," was in the making for the amphibious landing on Kyushu in the fall. It did not take much imagination to foresee that it would be a bloody engagement that would cost tens of thousands of lives.

During the summer of 1945, rumors circulated among some officers of the Third Fleet that Army Air Force pilots were making big bets that the war would be over in thirty or sixty days. It was ridiculous. The Japanese were not ready to give up. Navy men looked upon these harebrained stories as another example of wild Army pilots throwing their money away.

The Army pilots were not so wild. On August 6 at 0815, a bomb dropped on the city of Hiroshima from the B-29 *Enola Gay*, flying at an altitude of 31,600 feet. Until then, Hiroshima on the southeast coast of Honshu had been almost untouched by the war. The fireball ended the lives of one hundred thousand or possibly two hundred thousand human beings.

Men aboard the ships at sea soon learned the startling news that the war had taken a sudden turn and could end at any time. This new, unheard-of bomb took even the admirals by surprise. They had known nothing about this new weapon. The bomb was called an "atomic" bomb.

President Truman, returning from the Potsdam summit

conference on the cruiser *Augusta,* received the information that the bomb had been dropped in keeping with the order that he had approved. He told all hands on the ship, "This is the greatest thing in history." It was certainly the most awesome thing in history.

No one knew exactly what would happen now. The carrier strikes continued, but for how long? On August 9, as though nothing had changed, strong strikes were flown against northern Honshu and about four hundred enemy planes were destroyed or damaged on the ground. That same day a kamikaze crashed into the stern of the destroyer *Borie* and killed forty-eight men. It was also the same day that a second atomic bomb dropped on Nagasaki, the most Christian city in Japan. Set on hills, it reminded tourists of San Francisco. Now, the bombardier of the B-29 *Bock's Car* triggered the devastation of a city and its thousands of occupants. Perhaps seventy-five thousand were dead. No one really knew.

Still, the carrier strikes went on. On August 14, at 0415, strikes from TF38 against Tokyo began again. At 0615, the first planes were over the city and a second wave approached the coast. As they winged their way toward their targets, Halsey received an urgent message from Nimitz to suspend air operations. The Emperor had promised to surrender.

Halsey was impressed by an odd coincidence. On December 7, 1941, he was having breakfast on board the *Enterprise* when his flag secretary rushed in to tell him that Japan had attacked Pearl Harbor. Now, he received word that the war was over while having breakfast on the *Missouri.* The bearer of the news was the same man, Doug Moulton, who was now his air operations officer.

Halsey said that his first thought was "Victory. My second thought was, God be thanked, I'll never have to order another man out to die!"

McCain recalled the strikes that had been launched and canceled all others. Unfortunately, the first strike of six Hellcats from the *Yorktown* was jumped over Tokurozama airfield by fifteen or twenty enemy planes at exactly that time. Four Hellcats were lost.

All offensive operations against Japan ceased. Nimitz' top secret, highest priority message read:

CINCPAC: AIR ATTACK WILL BE SUSPENDED X ACKNOWLEDGE.

The fighting ended officially. Even then, some enemy planes attacked TF38, but they were quickly driven off or extinguished.

It was a fast end to a long war. September 2, 1945, was set as the day for the formal surrender.

From the time of the ceasefire on August 15 to the formal surrender on September 2, carrier planes enthusiastically took off to search for prisoner of war camps in Japan. Scouts ranged far and wide over the country, spotted prisons, and then bombers dropped medicine, food, and other necessities. This enjoyable task of finding and then helping those who had suffered so much became great sport. It continued until occupation troops could reach the camps.

Carrier pilots had strict orders not to land in Japan except for an emergency. Curiosity was too much for such daring pilots. Soon "forced" landings became so prevalent that it was claimed that they congested Atsugi airport. One thing is certain. When the Army Air Force planes landed at Atsugi on August 28, they were met by a large sign painted on the hangars:

WELCOME TO THE U.S. ARMY
FROM THE THIRD FLEET.

Early on September 2, 1945, a gray Sunday, Vice Admiral Wilkinson led a long procession of ships of the Third Amphibious Force into Tokyo Bay and landed the 1st Cavalry Division. At the same time, surrender ceremonies were underway on board Halsey's flagship *Missouri*. The name of the ship was fortunate since it was the home state of the new President.

Allied leaders gathered on the deck of the battleship to participate in the formalities. After the Japanese Foreign Minister Mamoru Shigemitsu, dressed in a tail coat and spats, and General Yoshijiro Umezu, chief of the Army general staff, and three representatives each from the Foreign Office, Army, and Navy arrived, the proceedings began.

General MacArthur came out on deck with Admirals Nimitz and Halsey. The general made a brief speech expressing the hope that "a better world shall emerge out of the blood and carnage of the past." Alongside him were two former prisoners of war, Lieutenant General Jonathan Wainwright, who had taken MacArthur's place early in the war and surrendered in the Philippines, and Lieutenant General Sir Arthur Perceval, who had surrendered Singapore.

The general motioned to the Japanese to come forward to sign the surrender document. The foreign minister was first. MacArthur said abruptly to his chief of staff, "Sutherland, show him where to sign."

General MacArthur signed the acceptance and Admirals Nimitz, Halsey, and Forrest Sherman signed as supporters.

Then, the allied representatives signed for their respective nations.

When the signatures were completed, MacArthur said, "Let us pray that peace be now restored to the world and that God will preserve it always. These proceedings are now closed."

In a few austere minutes, the war that had seemed everlasting was over. At that moment, hundreds of carrier and Army Air Force planes flew over the United States Fleet in Tokyo Bay. The carriers, still standing guard, were off the coast.

General Tojo, the former premier of Japan, said that one of the major reasons for the defeat of his country was the Fast Carrier Task Force. The theory of flexibility and mobility had worked and under the leadership of Mitscher the force had become unstoppable. The carrier, not the battleship, was now the strength of the fleet. TF58 and TF38 had become symbols of power.

The fast carriers had affected almost every phase of the war. They had blocked enemy expansion and led the attack on Japan. They had sunk more warships than any other part of the Navy and, second to submarines, sunk vast amounts of merchant shipping that helped destroy the enemy economy. And the Navy had established itself as the world's leading expert in precision bombing.

The war had been a series of contradictions that brought out the best and worst in men. The virtues of the men of the Fast Carrier Task Force were genuine. There was nothing false about their selflessness, daring, and courage in serving their nation's cause. The shame is that so much good had gone into such a destructive mission.

177

Commanders

LEADING AMERICAN NAVAL COMMANDERS

Admiral Ernest J. King, Chief of Naval Operations

Admiral Chester W. Nimitz, Commander-in-Chief United States Pacific Fleet

Admiral Raymond A. Spruance, Commander Fifth Fleet

Admiral William F. Halsey, Commander Third Fleet

Admiral Thomas C. Kinkaid, Commander Seventh Fleet

Vice Admiral Marc A. Mitscher, Commander Fast Carrier Force

Vice Admiral John S. McCain, Commander Fast Carrier Force

Vice Admiral Richmond K. Turner, Commander Fifth Amphibious Force

Vice Admiral Theodore S. Wilkinson, Commander Third Amphibious Force

LEADING JAPANESE NAVAL COMMANDERS

Admiral Isoroku Yamamoto, Commander-in-Chief of the Combined Fleet

Admiral Mineichi Koga, succeeded Yamamoto as Commander-in-Chief of the Combined Fleet

Admiral Soemu Toyoda, succeeded Koga as Commander-in-Chief of the Combined Fleet

Vice Admiral Jisaburo Ozawa, Commander of Mobile Fleet; and the "Main Body" at the battle for Leyte Gulf

Vice Admiral Takeo Kurita, Commander First Striking Force

Vice Admiral Shoji Nishimura, Commander Southern Force at the battle for Leyte Gulf

Carrier Strike Force

Vice Admiral Takijiro Onishi, Organizer of the Kamikaze Special Attack Corps

Vice Admiral Shigeru Fukudome, Naval Air Commander in the Philippines and Formosa

Vice Admiral Seichi Ito, Commander of the Surface Special Attack Unit

Carriers

SOME OUTSTANDING AIRCRAFT CARRIERS IN THE PACIFIC—WORLD WAR II

CV2	*Lexington*		CV12	*Hornet* (2nd)
CV3	*Saratoga*		CV13	*Franklin*
CV5	*Yorktown*		CV16	*Lexington* (2nd)
CV6	*Enterprise*		CV17	*Bunker Hill*
CV7	*Wasp*		CV18	*Wasp* (2nd)
CV8	*Hornet*		CVL22	*Independence*
CV9	*Essex*		CVL23	*Princeton*
CV10	*Yorktown* (2nd)		CVL24	*Belleau Wood*
CV11	*Intrepid*			

SOME ACTIVE JAPANESE AIRCRAFT CARRIERS

Amagi	*Ryuho*
Chitose	*Shokaku*
Chiyoda	*Taiho*
Hiyo	*Zuiho*
Junyo	*Zuikaku*
Katsuragi	

Hyuga—Hybrid battleship/carrier
Ise—Hybrid battleship/carrier

Major Operations

MAJOR OPERATIONS IN THE CENTRAL PACIFIC

The Gilbert Islands

Fast Carrier Strikes—1 September to 6 October 1943
Makin—19 to 29 November 1943
Tarawa—19 to 23 November 1943

The Marshall Islands

Kwajalein—31 January to 7 February 1944
Eniwetok—31 January to 4 March 1944

Truk

Fast Carrier Strikes—17 to 18 February 1944

Palau, Hollandia, Truk

Fast Carrier Strikes—22 March to 30 April 1944
Palau—15 September 1944

Marianas

Fast Carrier Strikes—11 to 13 June 1944
Saipan—15 to 21 June 1944
Tinian—24 July to 1 August 1944
Guam—21 July to 10 August 1944

Battle of the Philippine Sea

3 May to 24 June 1944

Okinawa and Formosa

Fast Carrier Strikes—10 to 14 October 1944

The Battle for Leyte Gulf

Leyte Landing—20 October 1944
24 to 26 October 1944

Lingayen Gulf

Fast Carrier Strikes—10 December 1944 to 10 January 1945
Landing—9 January 1945

South China Sea

Fast Carrier Strikes—10 to 20 January 1945

Formosa

Fast Carrier Strikes—20 to 27 January 1945

Iwo Jima

Fast Carrier Strikes—21 February to 1 March 1945

Okinawa

Fast Carrier Strikes Against Kyushu—18 to 31 March 1945
Landing—1 April 1945
Fast Carrier Support—April to May 1945
Fast Carrier Strikes Against Kyushu—15 to 16 April 1945
Fast Carrier Strikes Against Kyushu and Shikoku—12 to 13
   May 1945

Japan

Fast Carrier Strikes—2 June to 15 August 1945

Bibliography

*Blair, Clay, Jr., *Combat Patrol*, New York, Bantam Books, 1978.

Buell, Thomas B., *The Quiet Warrior*, Boston, Little Brown, 1974.

Clark, J. J., with Clark Reynolds, *Carrier Admiral*, New York, David McKay, 1967.

*Halsey, William F. and J. Bryan III, *Admiral Halsey's Story*, New York, McGraw-Hill, 1947.

* Ireland, Bernard, *The Aircraft Carrier: An Illustrated History*, Great Britain, Chartwell Books, 1979.

King, Ernest, and Walter M. Whitehill, *Fleet Admiral King*, New York, W. W. Norton, 1952.

Morison, Samuel E., *History of the United States Naval Operations in World War II*, 15 vols., Boston, Little Brown, 1948–1960.

Polamar, Norman, *Aircraft Carriers*, New York, Doubleday, 1969.

Reynolds, Clark G., *The Fast Carriers*, New York, McGraw-Hill, 1968.

Sherman, Frederick C., *Combat Command*, New York, E. P. Dutton, 1950.

*Smith, S. E., *The United States Navy in World War II*, New York, William Morrow, 1966.

*Stafford, Edward B., *The Big E*, New York, Random House, 1962.

Taylor, Theodore, *The Magnificent Mitscher*, New York, W. W. Norton, 1954.

*Toland, John, *The Rising Sun*, New York, Random House, 1970.

*Wilmott, H. P. *Warships*, London, Octopus Books, 1975.

Woodward, C. Vann, *The Battle for Leyte Gulf*, New York, Ballantine Books, 1947.

* These books are easiest to read.

Index

Fast Carrier Task Force, U.S.:
in battle for Leyte Gulf, 83, 87, 88-104, *105*
in battle of Philippine Sea, 65-81
in Formosa attacks, 91, 92, 135-136
in Gilbert Islands attacks, 36-47
in Iwo Jima operation, 141-143
in Japan attacks, 137-139, 170-172, 174
kamikaze damage to, *see* Kamikaze
list of ships in, 181
in Marshall Islands campaign, 47-51
in Okinawa operation, 145-166
in Truk Island attacks, 51-52, 54-56, 58, 61-63
in typhoons, 119-128, 167-170
See also names of ships; place names; Task Forces 15, 38, 58; U.S. Pacific Fleet
Fifth Amphibious Force, U.S., 64, 83
Fifth Fleet, U.S., 64, 118, 136
in Okinawa operation, 145, 158
Fighter (U.S. plane), 29, 30, 33, 39, 52, 54, 58, 64, 76, 83, 101, 112-113, 138
Formosa, 14, 130
U.S. attacks on, 89, 91, 92, 95, 129, 135-136
Franklin (U.S. ship), 92, *93*, 118, 147, 148, 151, 152
Fukodome, Vice Admiral Shigeru, 91, 92

Gilbert Islands, U.S. attacks on, 36-47
Guadalcanal, 9, 11
Guam, 10, 57, 65, 68, 73, 167

Halsey, Admiral William, 16, 48, 50, 82, 83, *84*, 117, 118, 164, 165, 166, 176
in battle for Leyte Gulf, 85-87, 89, 90, 94, 97, 98, 100-103, 105, 108-110, 114-116
in Formosa attacks, 129, 135-136
in Japan attacks, 170, 171, 174
in typhoons, 119-122, 126, 127, 167, 170
Hellcat (U.S. plane), *28*, 29, 30, 36, 46, 52, 54, 58, 64, 68, 71, 75, 77, 83, 140, 175
Helldiver (U.S. plane) 32, 77, 79, 83, 140
Hiroshima, 170, 173, 174
Hiyo (Jap. ship), 73, 77, 78
Hollandia, 88, 89, 90
Honshu Island, U.S. attacks on, 170, 171, 174
Hornet (U.S. ship), 9-10, 11, 30, 48, 68, 73, 86, 137, 169
Hyuga (Jap. ship), 97, 135, 146, 171

Independence (U.S. ship), 14, 35, 42, 83, 121
Intrepid (U.S. ship), 52, 54, 55, 83, 101, 118, 145
Ise (Jap. ship), 97, 135, 146, 171
Ito, Vice Admiral Seichi, 153, 155
Iwo Jima, U.S. attacks on, 65, 137, 139-143

Japan, U.S. attacks on, 137-139, 170-172, 174
Japanese Fleet:
kamikazes and, *see* Kamikaze
list of carriers in, 181
major operations with U.S. Fast Carrier Task Force, 183-184 (*see also place names*)

188

190

ous Force; Fifth Fleet; PT
boats; Seventh Fleet; Task
Forces 15, 38, 58; Third Amphibious Force; Third Fleet

Wake Island, 10, 34, 35, 36
Wasp (U.S. ship), 1, 73, 117,
121, 146-147, *149*, 151
Wilkinson, Vice Admiral Theodore, 83, 86, 89, 134, 176

Yap Island, 86, 87

Yorktown (U.S. ship), 11, *23*, *28*,
35, 42-44, 46, 52, 59, 62, 68,
145, 175

Zeke (Jap. plane), 52, 54, 58, 62,
115, 129-130, 157, 161
Zero (Jap. plane), 29, 68, 69, 71,
73, 77
Zuiho (Jap. ship), 68, 116
Zuikaku (Jap. ship), 69, 75, 78,
116

About the Author

Ernest A. McKay teaches American and aviation history at the State University of New York—Maritime College. He is a graduate of Colgate University with a Ph.D. in history from New York University. During World War II, he served with the Third Amphibious Force in the Pacific and participated in landings at Leyte and Lingayen Gulf, and the battle for Leyte Gulf. During the Korean conflict he was a Lieutenant Commander, USNR, on the staff of the Under Secretary of the Navy. He is the author of numerous articles and three other books; the most recent, A World to Conquer, is about the first world flight in 1924.